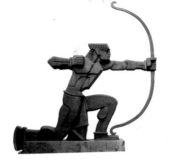

LONDON
ART DECO

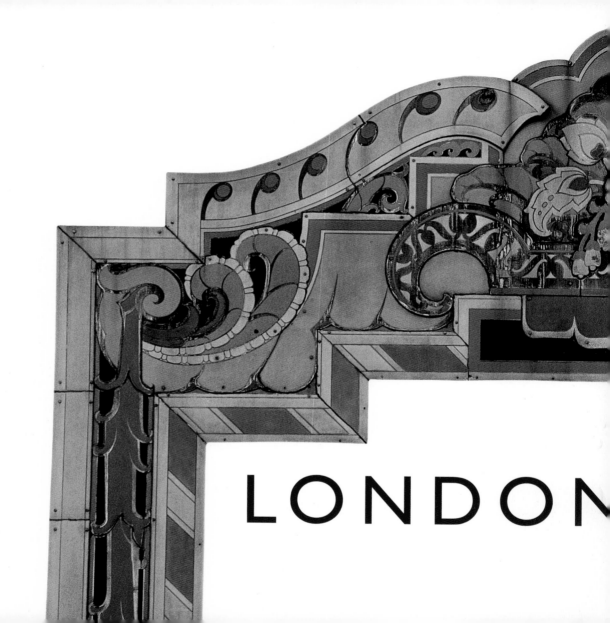

LONDON

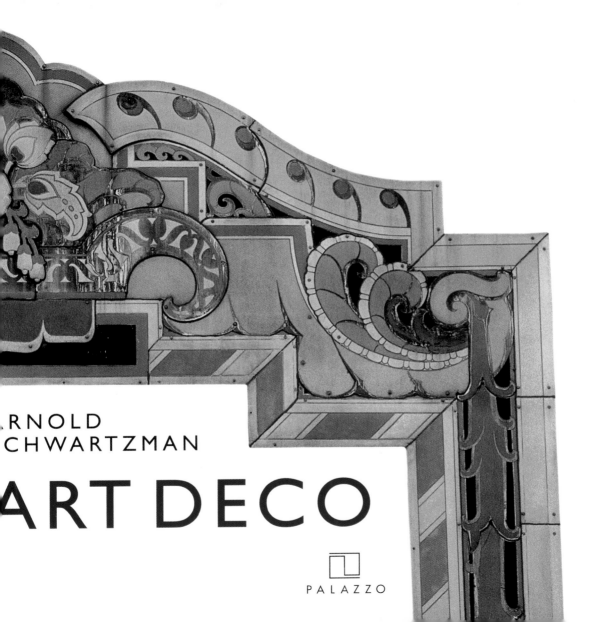

ARNOLD
SCHWARTZMAN

ART DECO

PALAZZO

Half title:
East Finchley
Underground Station,
1940.
Great North Road, N2.
'Archie',
a three-dimensional sculpture.
Sculptor: Eric Aumonier.

Title page:
Ideal House,
National Radiator
Building, 1928.
Great Marlborough Street
and Argyle Street.
Detail, enamel on
bronze decoration by
The Birmingham Guild
of Handicraft.
Architects:
Raymond M. Hood
and Gordon Jeeves.

This revised edition published in 2013 by
PALAZZO EDITIONS LTD
15 Church Road,
London SW13 9HE
United Kingdom

www.palazzoeditions.com

Design, text and photographs copyright
© 2013 Arnold Schwartzman

Design by Arnold Schwartzman
Art Production by Isolde Schwartzman

A CIP catalogue record for this book is available from
the British Library.

ISBN 9780957148321

5 6 7 8

Printed and bound in China by Imago.

Acknowledgments

Dedicated to the citizens and artisans of London.

With special thanks to my wife and partner, Isolde, for her
excellent production skills and patience, and to our editor
Victoria Webb at Palazzo Editions.

I further wish to thank the following for their
invaluable assistance:
Associated Newspapers Limited
Michael Beavan, Maybourne Group
Pam Carter, The Savoy
Gill Christophers, Claridge's
Tim Clark, MA RIBA
Gregory de Clerck, Park Lane Hotel –
    Starwood Hotels and Resort
Jo Darke, Public Sculpture and
    Monument Association
Goldman Sachs International
Tony Graves,
    Hammersmith Hospitals NHS Trust
Lisa Meacock,
    Royal Institute of British Architects
Professor Douglas Merritt, ARCA FSCD
Ave Pildas
Hannah Schwartzman
John and Sheila Tribe
Diana and Ivan Ziekenoppasser

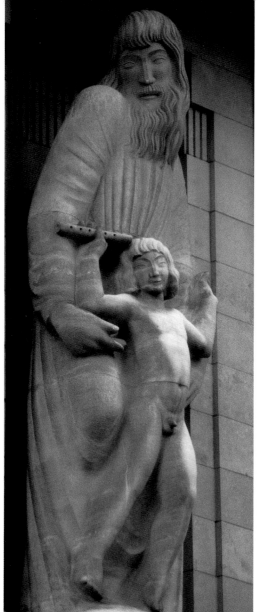

Contents

BBC Broadcasting House, 1931–32. Portland Place, W1. *Sculptural figures above the main entrance shows 'Prospero, Ariel's master, sending him out into the world', prior to recent restoration.* Sculptor: Eric Gill.

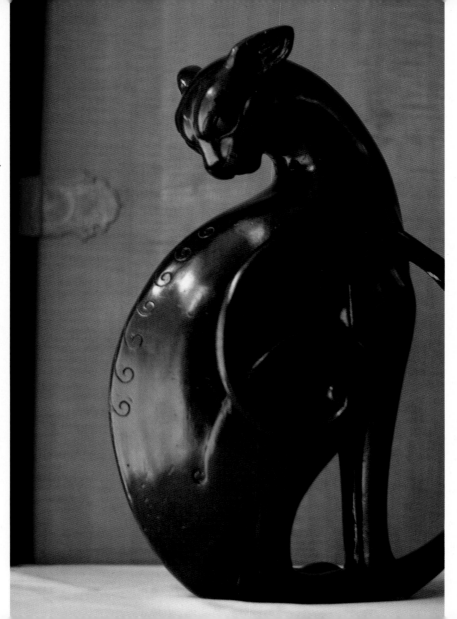

The Savoy, 1889.
Strand, WC2.
'Kaspar the Cat', 1926.
Just before leaving for
South Africa, Woolf Joel
gave a dinner party for 14
at The Savoy. One guest
cancelled at the last minute,
but the host baulked at the
superstition that whoever
left the table first would be
destined to die first. A few
weeks later, Woolf was shot
dead in his office. Since
then, if there happened to
be 13 guests at a party,
a member of staff would
be recruited to join them,
but this was sometimes
inconvenient when the
company wanted to discuss
private matters. To solve the
problem, Basil Ionides was
commissioned to design a
cat, christened Kaspar,
which he carved from a
single piece of planetree.
If a party of 13 is dining
at The Savoy, Kaspar is
placed on the 14th chair
with a napkin tied around
his neck and is treated as
a bona fide guest.
Sculptor: Basil Ionides.

Introduction

'THINGS TO COME', the film adaptation of H.G. Wells' book, and Charlie Chaplin's *Modern Times*, both released in 1936, were depictions of the future and of mankind coping with the machine age, of which Karl Marx proclaimed that man is a 'mere appendage to the machine'. That same year, 1936, the year of my birth, also saw the launch of British television, the maiden voyages of the Hindenberg airship and the RMS Queen Mary, as well as the design of London Film Productions' laboratories by Bauhaus architect Walter Gropius, with Maxwell Fry.

Art Deco reflected the new industrial age and embraced all forms of design, not least that of architecture, drawing from a variety of influences including ancient Egyptian, Moorish and Mayan motifs and the Cubism, Fauvism and *De Stijl* movements.

The Art Deco style gained prominence at the 1925 *Exposition Internationale des Artes Decoratifs et Industriels* in Paris, where one French critic disdainfully described the British Pavilion as 'a fantasy... designed by a retired colonel', presumably referring to Lt. Col. G. Val Myer, one of the architects of the BBC's Broadcasting House. When it was built in 1932, the *Architectural Review* described the BBC Headquarters as parting the road 'like a battleship floating towards the observer' – its later war-time camouflage further enforced this perception.

The technical director of the British Pavilion at the Paris 1925 exhibition was Oliver Bernard, responsible for the design of the Lyons Corner Houses and the J. Lyons Group of hotels, notably the Strand Palace, 1930. Other prime examples of London's hotels of the era include the Grosvenor House, Dorchester, Mount Royal and Park Lane.

In the wake of the Paris exhibition, Art Deco became the first truly international style, quickly spreading around the world. Each nation seemed to adapt its own distinct architectural style. Less florid than the French or that of the United States, Great Britain's buildings reflected the country's imperial status and the national love of architectural detail. In London, in particular, Art Deco quickly became the style of choice for a succession of landmark buildings. Growing up in the Capital, these treasures surrounded me and had a profound and lasting influence on my life.

As a child, my parents would take me on regular annual treats, in winter to Bertram Mills' Circus at Olympia Exhibition Halls (1929–30), the Empire's largest building, with its name in huge cast concrete sans serif letters, and in the summer to Regent's Park Zoo, where my favourite enclosure was the Streamline Moderne penguin pool (1935).

'Let's all go down the Strand...' My father, a waiter at the famed Savoy Hotel, would occasionally take

'Let's all go down the Strand!' (Popular British Music Hall song.) '...Let's all go down the Strand! I'll be the leader, you can march behind. Come with me and see what we can find! Let's all go down the Strand!...'

Wandsworth Town Hall, 1930–37.
Wandsworth High Street and Fairfield Street, SW18.
Bricklayer with trowel. 'Housing', one of a pair of Portland stone lintels.
Sculptor: David Evans.
Architect: Edward A. Hunt, JP FRIBA.

A bas-relief frieze running the length of the Town Hall represents the history of the five parishes which make up the former metropolitan borough of Wandsworth.

me on the No. 31 double-decker tram car 'up west.' It was an exciting experience rattling down Holborn's Kingsway tunnel to emerge a few minutes later into the bright sunlight filtering through the amber window at the front of the tram. Arriving at the Thames-side Victoria Embankment we would alight at Cleopatra's Needle, where I would gaze up at the enormous clock of the Shell-Mex Company building, appropriately dubbed by A.P. Herbert as 'Big Benzine'.

Climbing up the Savoy Steps we would stop off briefly at the hotel's kitchens, where I was offered treats such as Peach Melba and privileged to stroke the hotel's legendary sleek black 'Kaspar the Cat', then we would continue along the Strand, past the imposing courtyard of the Savoy with its shiny stainless steel canopy, and the adjoining Savoy Theatre designed by Basil Ionides in 1939. On the opposite side of the road stands the Strand Palace Hotel, where our faces would positively glow from the glass-panelled balustrades in its beautiful lobby, which have only recently re-emerged at the Victoria & Albert Museum's 2003 Art Deco exhibition.

Walking further down the Strand, we would pass a myriad of examples of Art Deco architecture: the Shell-Mex building and its adjacent sculpture-covered New Adelphi, the black imitation marble Adelphi Theatre (1930), and Halifax House (1933).

On reaching the Lyons Corner House for afternoon tea, we would cross the plush deco pattern carpet to our table set with stylish plates, honey pot and silver toast rack, to be served by 'Nippies' in their starched white pinnies and head-bands. In the background, a palm court orchestra played popular tunes of the day. From Trafalgar Square, with its newly sculpted fountains by Sir Charles Wheeler and W. McMillan, we could see the new imposing Commonwealth headquarters representing Great Britain's far-flung empire.

We continued our leisurely strolls down Whitehall, past the Whitehall Theatre (1930). On reaching Sir Edwin Lutyen's Portland stone Cenotaph Memorial (1920), my father would respectfully raise his trilby. The Cenotaph's stepped design was echoed in King George V's elegant Empire Walnut microphone made for His Majesty's speech to the Empire, broadcast by the BBC in 1932.

After the First World War, the British government had implemented a work programme similar to U.S. President Roosevelt's Works Progress Administration (WPA). The initiative spawned a slew of civic

8

centres throughout the metropolis, including the town halls of Brixton, Greenwich, Hammersmith, Hornsey, Walthamstow and Wandsworth. Sculptural images of workers with trowels, picks, pneumatic drills, sledgehammers, spanners, shovels, anvils and scythes, appeared on many of London's buildings, a tribute to the labour force assisting the country to get back on its feet, as can still be seen at The Royal Institute of British Architects' fine building, resplendent with its overall craftsmanship and design.

Benjamin Disraeli said 'London is a modern Babylon'. In stark contrast to these mostly Portland stone buildings is the black granite and Persian-style decoration of the National Radiator Company's Ideal House (1928). Reflected in its shiny façade is Liberty's department store, which although a contemporary structure (1924–26), was built in half-timbered Tudor style. Ideal House, designed by American architect Raymond Hood, was referred to as 'bad taste', by the *Architectural Review*, and the Royal Institute of British Architects's President called it 'foreign'. Alien influences did indeed come with the influx of European emigré architects and designers prior to the Second World War, who infused a new spirit of design into the British nation.

Along the strip of the Great West Road known as the 'Golden Mile' are located a number of Art Deco factories. Sadly the dazzling Firestone Tyre and Rubber Company building (1929), was demolished just one day prior to its preservation order being enacted. Other close-by gems are the Coty, Pyrene, Gillette, and Hoover buildings. Architectural critic Nikolaus Pevsner described the latter as 'perhaps the most offensive of the modernistic atrocities along this road of typical By-Pass factories'.

Occasionally my mother would take me on shopping expeditions to Oxford Street, which was known as the 'Ladies Mile' due to the growing number of department stores: most prominent was Selfridges emporium and its ornate 'Queen of Time' clock designed by Gilbert Bayes. Adjacent was Lilley & Skinner's large shoe store, with its filigree Deco window grilles, where my feet, plus the new shoes, would be examined in the shop's state-of-the-art X-ray machine; however, the radiation was later found to have harmful effects.

In nearby Brook Street, Mayfair, is a Streamline clothing boutique designed by Sir John Burnet, and immediately opposite stand the 18th century former homes of George Friedrich Handel and his later

9

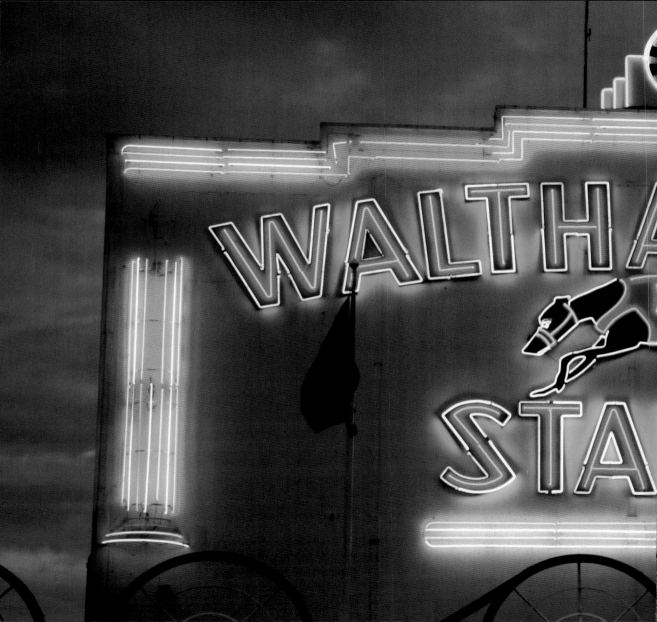

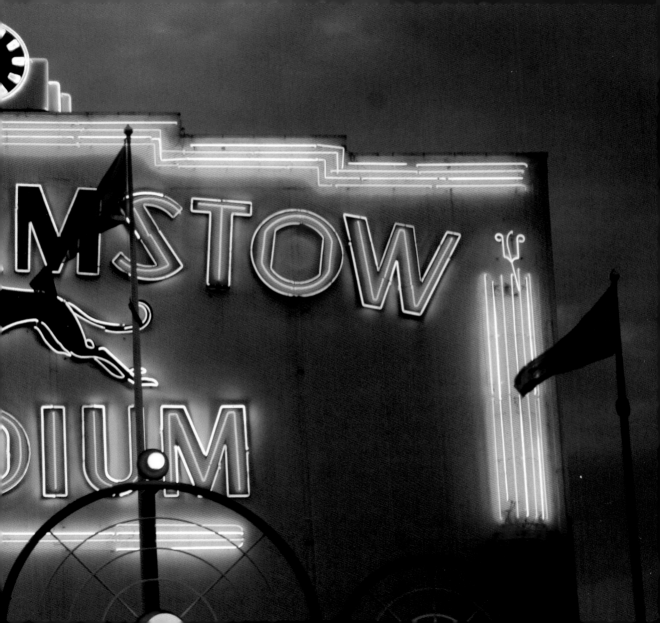

next-door neighbour, Jimi Hendrix, where they composed *The Messiah* and *Foxy Lady*, respectively. On the same side of the street is Claridge's hotel with its classic Deco interiors by Basil Ionides.

In Upper Brook Street, the seafaring Lord Louis Mountbatten had a 1930s-style pied-à-terre resembling a ship's cabin with portholes looking out onto a backcloth painted with a scene of Monte Carlo harbour. Luxury apartments, as well as Government subsidised housing flourished throughout the capital. Even the interior of Eltham Palace, the medieval former home of Henry VIII, was converted in 1936 into an Art Deco residence for art patron Stephen Courtauld and his wife, Virginia.

All this was a far cry from the drab surroundings of my birthplace in London's East End where, in 1940, on the first day of the London Blitz, our home was destroyed, including our cut-glass rose tinted mirrors, the Pye Model 'K' radio with its fretwork sunrise cabinet, and the cream and green tiled stepped fireplace.

Many of London's grandest architectural icons were demolished or damaged during the War, remarkably many did survive, including numerous movie houses. By 1932, London boasted over 250 cinemas. I recall visiting for sixpence the classic streamlined Victoria Station Newsreel Cinema, and the Art Deco 'Eros' in Piccadilly Circus. Eventually many of the picture palaces fell as casualties to the emergence of television and were either demolished or converted into bingo halls, churches and rock concert halls.

The Egyptian-style decorations of George Cole's Carlton Cinema, the 'Black Cat' cigarette factory, and Adelaide House, among other buildings, were inspired by the discovery of Tutankhamen's Tomb by Lord Carnarvon and Howard Carter in 1922.

After graduating from art school, followed by military service in Korea, I moved back to London, where I rented a flat directly opposite the New Victoria Theatre, with its imposing frontage displaying two large *lap* silvered bas-reliefs. Commuting on the Underground one day during the 1970s, I noticed that the beautiful bronze fluted uplights alongside the escalators were being removed, to be replaced by fluorescent tubing. On telephoning London Transport to enquire about the possibility of purchasing one, I was told that most of the opaque white glass shades had been broken, and the bronze was to be sold as scrap metal. Remaining examples still survive at Southgate Underground station.

Frank Pick, the design manager, who later became the Vice Chairman of the London Passenger Transport Board, commissioned Charles Holden to design the new LPTB headquarters (1927–29), as well as a great number of London Underground stations. Holden employed Eric Gill and Henry Moore, among others, to produce sculptures for the new building, and despite Pick's protestations, also asked Sir Jacob Epstein to create two major pieces, 'Day' and 'Night'. The results fuelled further controversy in the aftermath of the outrage caused by his design of 'Rima' for the Hudson Memorial. Pick also commissioned posters from the likes of Edward McKnight Kauffer, Edward Bawden and Frank Newbould, and a ground-breaking diagramatic Underground map by Henry C. Beck (1933).

In 1916, a special London Underground printing font designed by Edward Johnston was introduced. Johnston was Eric Gill's tutor at the Central School of Art. Gill later became the celebrated sculptor, lettercutter, and typeface designer. His fonts, Gill Sans and Perpetua, are used throughout this book.

Eric Aumonier's sculpture of an archer at East Finchley Underground Station (perhaps inspired by Alan Rogers' 1930 Underground poster 'Speed' featuring an image of an archer) points away from the Deco sunrises of suburbia to the splendors of central London's rich vein of Art Deco treasures dotted between the city's ancient monuments. Today, like the picture palaces, countless of these no longer serve their original purpose, such as the former London County Council headquarters, now a hotel and art gallery. Fleet Street newspaper buildings have been turned into financial institutions, a vacuum cleaner factory into a supermarket, garages into restaurants, a department store is a book store and a town hall is now a dance agency.

The Moderne-style Imperial Airways Terminal, now the National Audit Office, was conveniently situated adjoining the platform at Victoria Station that would take passengers by train to the new Croydon Airport or Southampton, to board their flying boats, or by coach from the Moderne Victoria Coach Station (1931–32), directly opposite.

'California Here I Come…' On a cold rainy morning in 1978, my wife and I left from the former Imperial Airways Terminal on our way to our new home in sunny California. As I gazed out of the coach window, beyond the many bowler-hatted commuters with their black umbrellas, I could see Sir Gilbert Scott's iconic Battersea Power Station's chimney stacks silhouetted against the grey sky, and began to feel like one of the saddened-faced subjects in Ford Madox Brown's painting, 'The Last of England'.

Fortunately it was not to be my last sighting of London, as over these past thirty years I have returned frequently to relish the rich architectural heritage of the time and place of my birth, of which I shall never tire.

'Carry On London!'

Arnold Schwartzman, Hollywood, 2006

'Carry On London!'
'In Town Tonight', the popular BBC weekly radio programme, launched in 1933, opened with 'Once again we silence the mighty roar of London's traffic to bring to the microphone some of the interesting people who are in town tonight!'. The programme signed off with 'Carry On London!'.

Overleaf:
"Music" and "Dance", two of several low reliefs by Eric Gill for the facade of Peoples Palace, 1936. Mile End Road, E1.

13

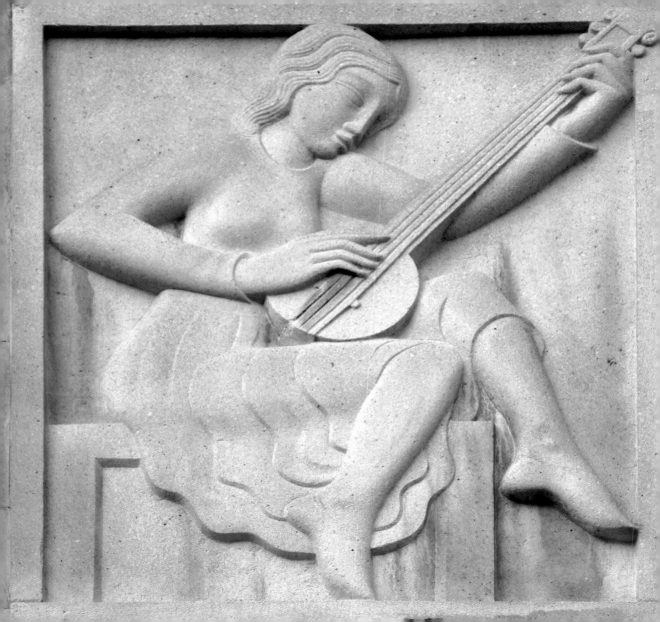

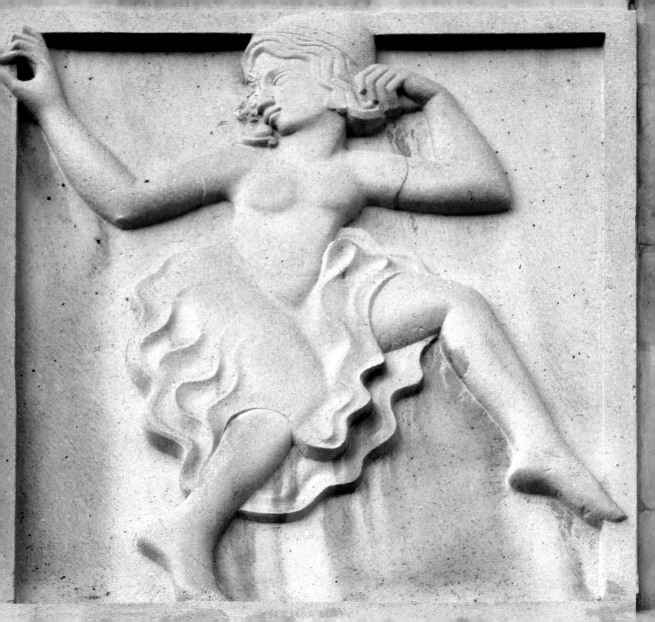

Corporate Buildings

Opposite:
Shell-Mex Company
building, 1931.
80 Strand and
Victoria Embankment,
WC2.
*Built on the former site
of the Hotel Cecil.
The ten-storey Portland
stone, 550,000 square feet
building is surmounted by
London's largest clock, which,
flanked by eight sculpted
figures, sits atop the
building like a giant
mantel clock.
The clock's simple
diamond-shaped markers
dispensed with Roman or
Egyptian numerals, which
can be read easily from
across the Thames.
This innovation prompted
the 1935 Joseph Lee
cartoon of two men
standing beneath the
Shell-Mex clock:
'Excuse me, but is that
blob minutes past
blob o'clock, or just blob
minutes to blob?'
Architects:
Messrs. Joseph.*

'FORGET SIX COUNTIES OVERHUNG WITH SMOKE…and dream of London, small and white.' — William Morris. The majority of London's major buildings constructed between the world wars were surfaced with Portland stone, an indigenous material found only on the isle of Portland in the county of Dorset. The white Oolitic limestone has graced the facades of the Capital's grandest buildings since the time of Inigo Jones and Sir Christopher Wren.

This precious stone was plagued by the 'London Particular' or 'Pea souper' as it was also known. This terrible smog produced mainly from domestic coal-burning fires, as well as those of industry, covered the snow-white Portland stone with layers of grime and soot.

That's Shell, That Was! Among the most prominent of these Portland stone buildings is the former headquarters of the Shell-Mex Company, which dominates a vista across the north bank of the Thames.

The BBC's Broadcasting House's facade has been recently restored to its former glory, displaying several fine sculptural reliefs by Eric Gill. When asked to produce representations of Prospero and Ariel, Gill mused 'very clever of the BBC to hit on the idea, Ariel and aerial. Ha!Ha!'.

'Out to tickle tired eyes', in contrast, are the black granite National Radiator's Ideal House and the vitrolite glass of the Daily Express building.

16

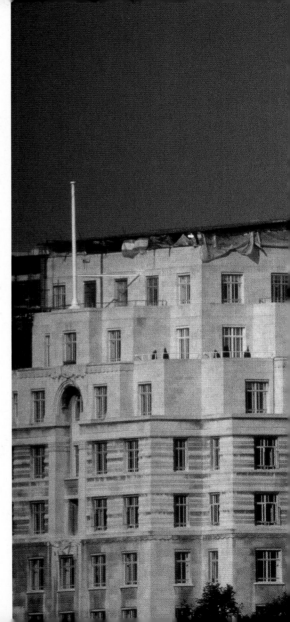

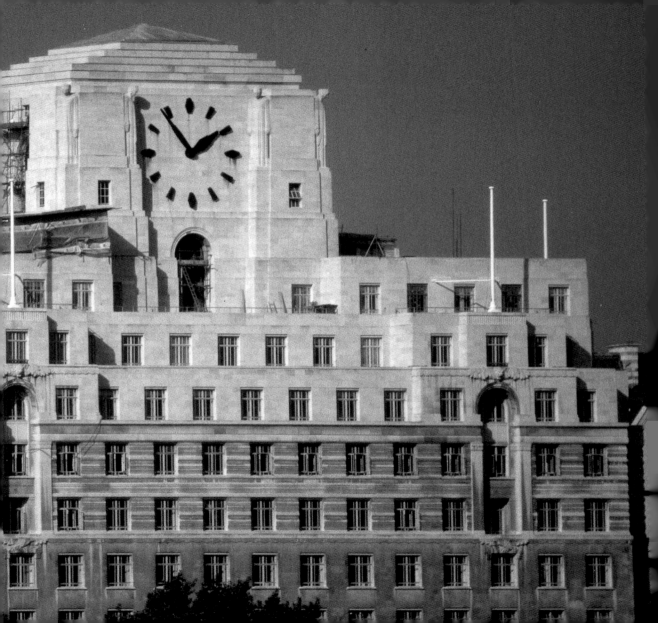

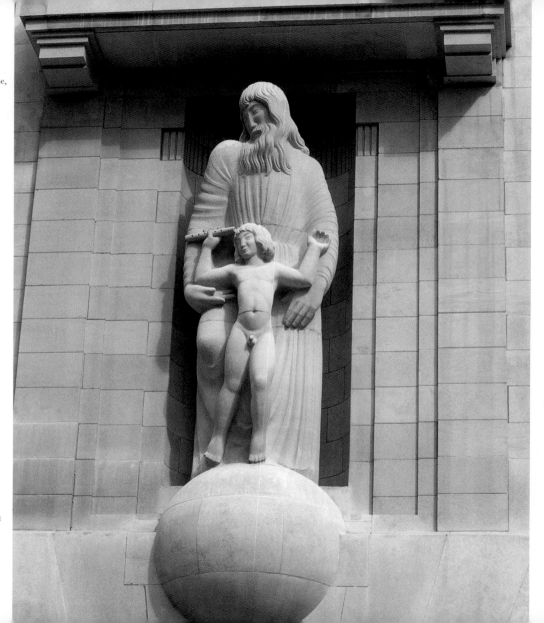

BBC Broadcasting House,
1931–32.
Portland Place, W1.
*Sculptural figures above
the main entrance shows
'Prospero, Ariel's master,
sending him out into
the world'.
The model for 'Ariel'
was well-known actor
Leslie French.*
Sculptor: Eric Gill.

18

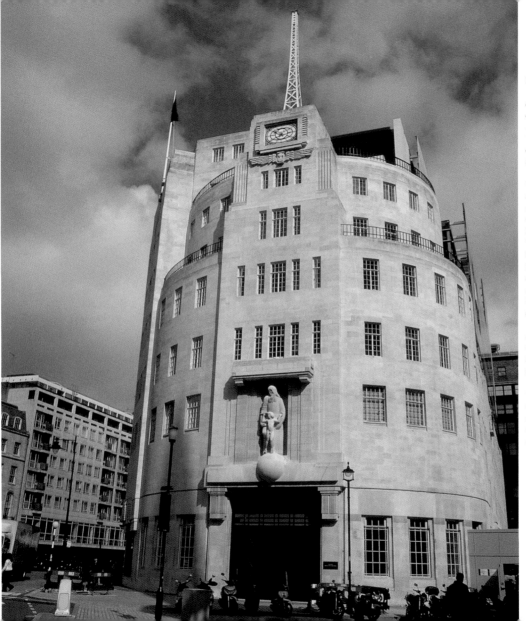

BBC Broadcasting House.
'The new Tower of London',
a nine-storey building, stands
on the former site of an
18th century manor house.
The BBC headquarters is
decorated with sculptures
including the BBC motto:
'Nation Shall Speak Peace
Unto Nation', by
Eric Gill and Vernon Hill,
with interior murals by
Gilbert Bayes.
Interior design:
Wells Coates,
Serge Chermayeff,
Raymond McGrath
and others.
Architects:
Lt. Col. G. Val Myer, RIBA.
and Watson-Hart.

In 1931, Wells Coates and
Chermayeff visited the
Dessau Bauhaus to study
the use of tubular steel.

The building's restoration,
completed in 2005, reveals the
original 78,000 cubic feet
of white Portland stone
in all its splendour.

19

Top:
BBC Broadcasting House.
Sculpted reliefs
'Ariel between
Wisdom and Gaiety'.
Sculptor: Eric Gill.

and below:
BBC Broadcasting House.
'Ariel hearing celestial music'.
Sculptor: Eric Gill.

Opposite:
BBC Broadcasting House.
'Ariel piping to children',
on the east side of the
building, a reference to the
BBC's *'Children's Hour'.*
Sculptor: Eric Gill.

Other works by Eric Gill
that can still be seen in
London include those at
London Transport Passenger
Board's Broadway House,
(pages 94, 95);
Bentall's department store,
Kingston-upon-Thames;
the 14 Stations of the Cross,
Westminster Cathedral,
Ashley Place, SW1;
and the People's Palace,
Mile End Road, E1,
a cultural and recreation
centre (now Queen Mary
and Westfield College),
has exterior reliefs depicting
Drama, Music, Brotherhood,
Dance and Sport.

20

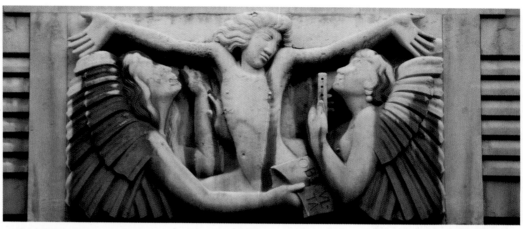

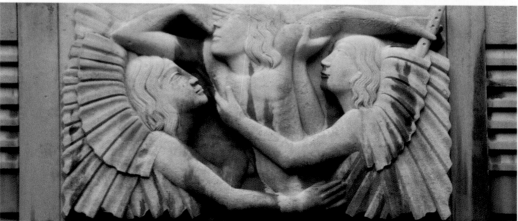

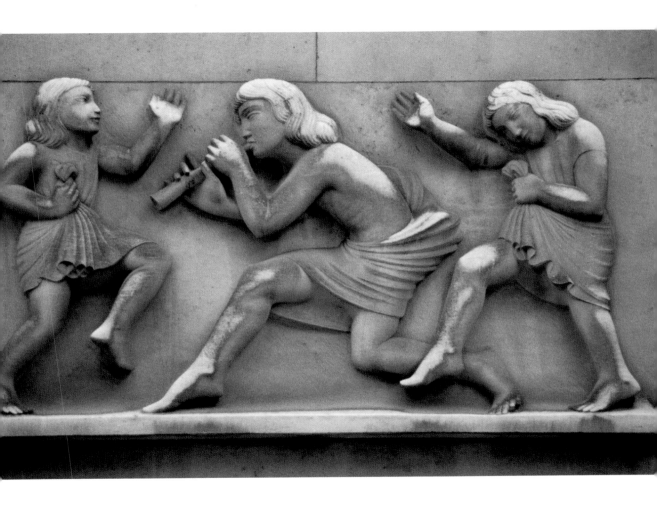

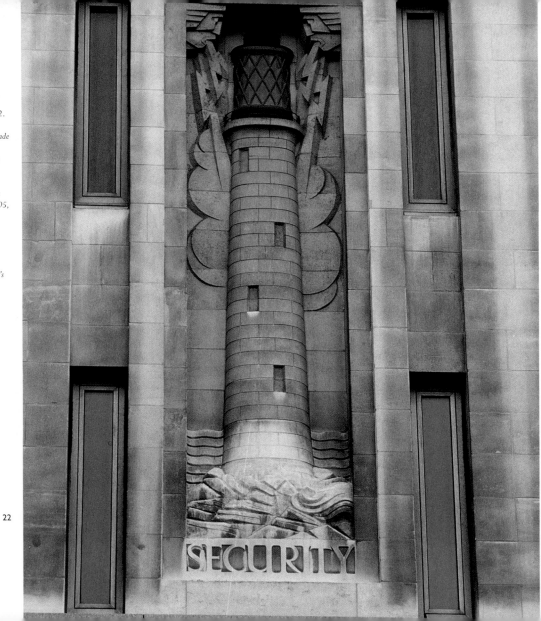

This page:
Abbey House,
Abbey National
Building Society, 1932.
Baker Street, W1.
Portland stone block façade
with an approximately
60-foot-high lighthouse
with intermittently
flashing lamp.
The structure underwent
major restoration in 2005,
to become residential
apartments and retail
at street level.
The building includes
the address of
Sir Arthur Conan Doyle's
fictitious detective
Sherlock Holmes,
221B Baker Street.
Architect: J.J. Joass.

Opposite:
Abbey House.
Portland stone
clock tower.

22

SECURITY

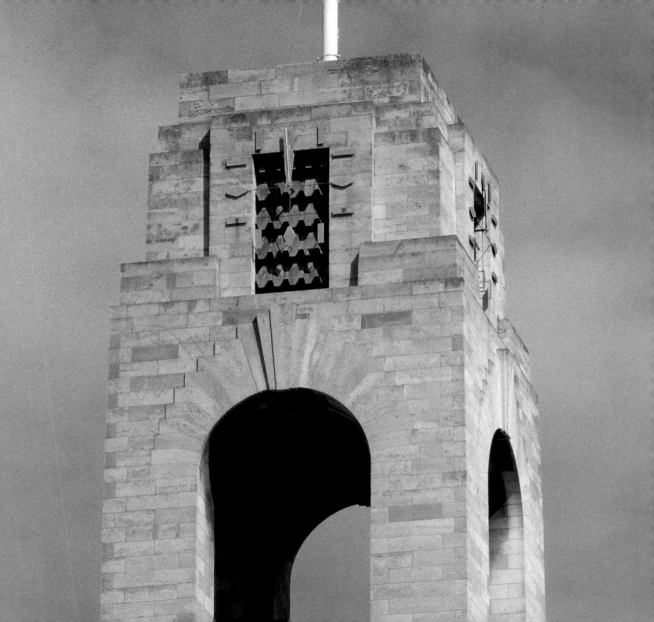

This page and opposite:
The New Adelphi, 1938.
Adam Street and
Victoria Embankment,
WC2.
*Several of a number of
Portland stone relief
sculptural vignettes on
an office building,
constructed on the site
of the original Adelphi
riverside apartment complex
which was demolished
in 1936.*
*Designed by the Adams
brothers (John, Robert and
William), 1768–72,
the building's name was
derived from 'Adelphoi'
the Greek word for brothers.*
Architects:
Messrs. Colcutt
and Hemp.

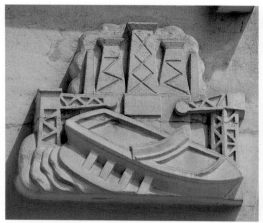
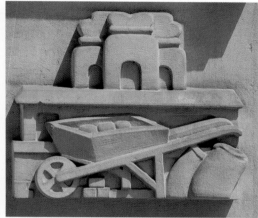
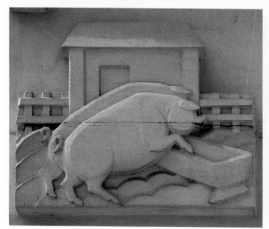
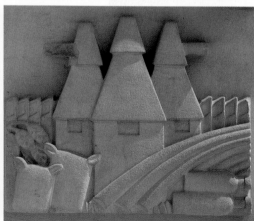

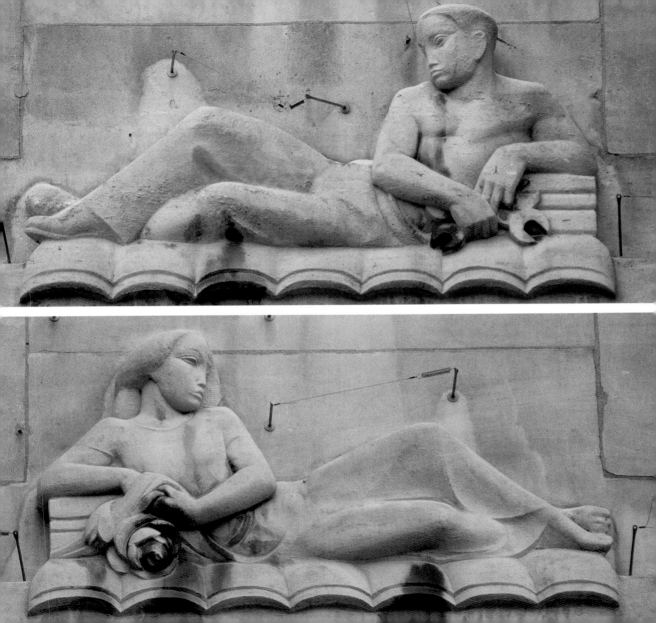

This page:
Adelaide House,
1920–25.
King William Street,
EC4.
*Built on the former site
of the Pearl Assurance
Company, Adelaide House
is located on the
bridgehead of
London Bridge.*
Architects:
Sir John Burnet Tait
and Partners.

Opposite:
Imperial Airways,
1937-39.
(Now the National
Audit Office)
157–197 Buckingham
Palace Road, SW1.
*'Wings over the World',
sculptural figures above
the former airline
terminal entrance.*
Sculptor:
E.R. Broadbent.
Architect:
Albert Lakeman.

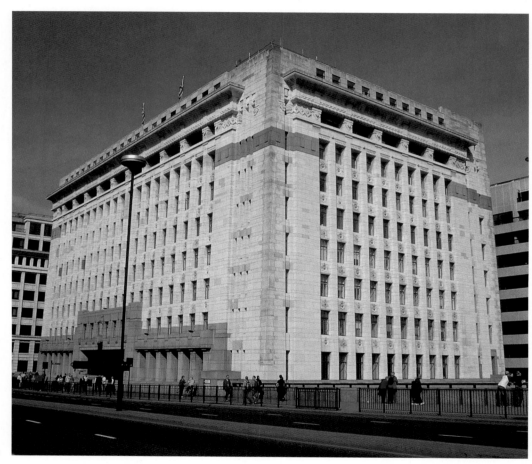

26

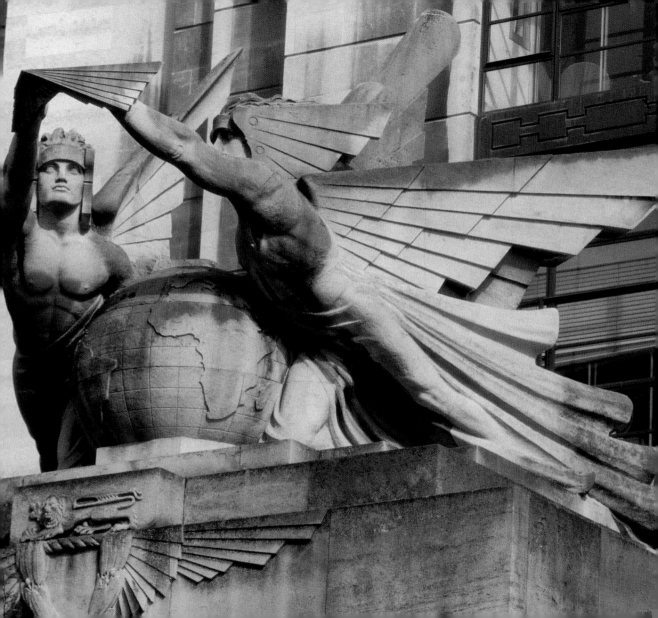

This page:
Holland House
(formerly W. H. Muller
Dutch shipping)
1-4 Bury Street,
EC3.
*Marble corner decoration
of a ship's prow.*
Architect: H. P. Belage
Sculptor:
J. Mendes da Costa.

Opposite:
Thornycroft House,
1920s.
Dean Bradley Street,
SW1.
*The Portland stone relief
panels reflect the activities
in which the original
occupants were engaged,
depicting lorries, trains,
steamers and warships,
superimposed upon an
image of Vulcan, god of
smiths.*

*Sir John Isaac Thornycroft
was the founder of the
Thornycroft shipbuilding
company. There were two
separate firms: one naval
and the other making steam
powered lorries plus more
conventional transport.*

28

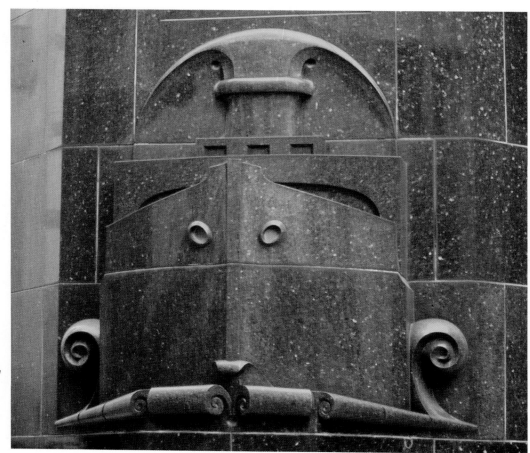

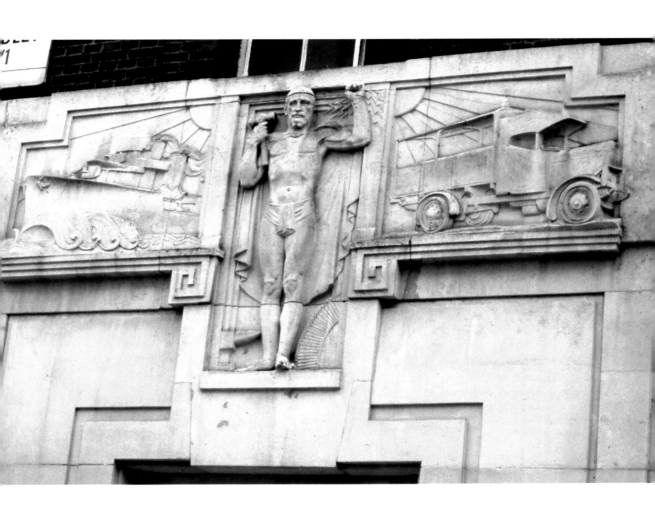

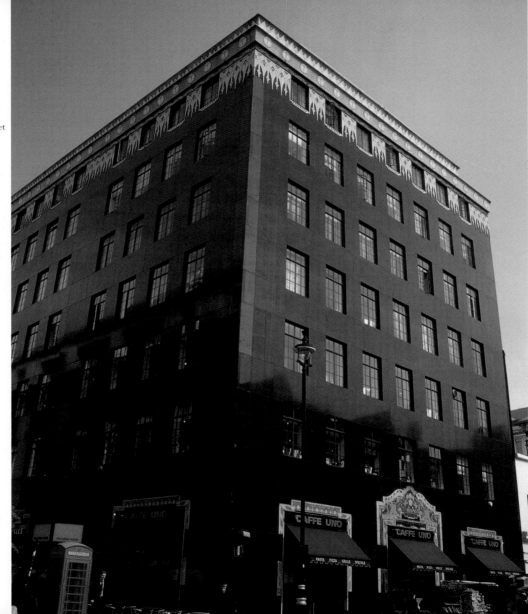

This page and opposite:
Ideal House, National
Radiator Building, 1928.
(Now Palladium House)
Great Marlborough Street
and Argyle Street, W1.
*Dubbed 'The Moor of
Argyle Street', Ideal House
is clad in shiny black
granite, with
Persian-style enamel
on bronze decoration by
The Birmingham Guild
of Handicraft.*
Architects:
Raymond M. Hood
with additions by
Gordon Jeeves, 1935.

30

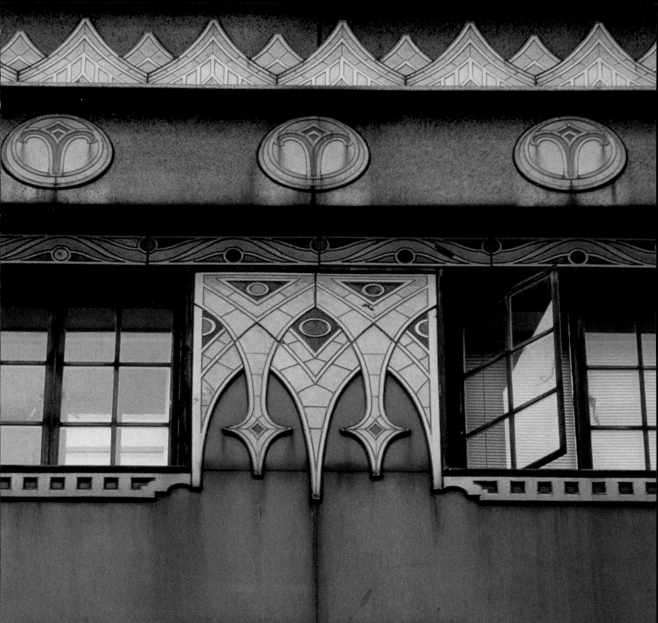

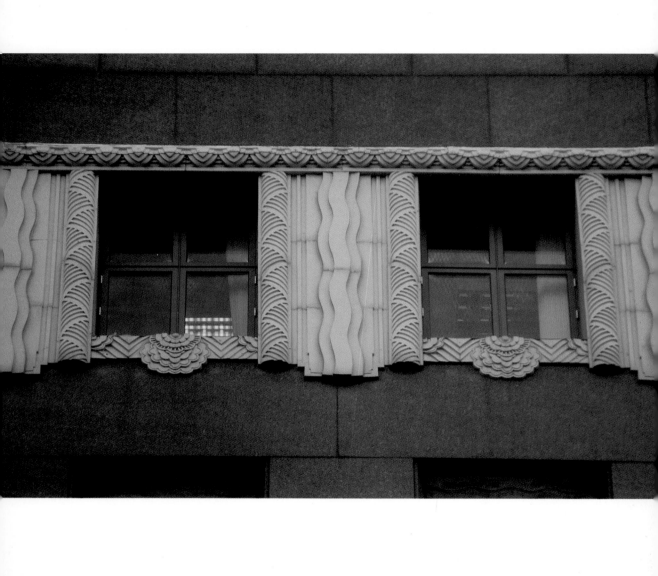

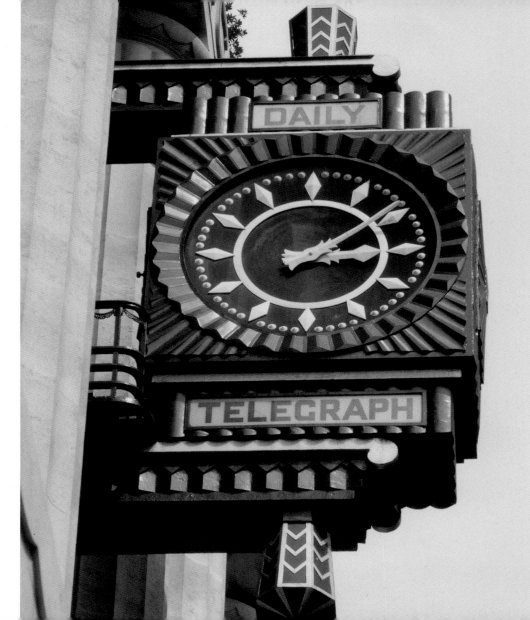

Opposite:
Gainsborough House, 1929.
81 Oxford Street, W1.
Glazed facing and pink decoration around the windows.
Architects:
S. Gordon Jeeves and Herbert A. Welch.

This page:
Daily Telegraph newspaper building, 1928.
(Now Goldman Sachs International),
120 Fleet Street, EC4.
Clock above the entrance of the stepped Portland stone façade.
Architects:
Elcock and Sutcliffe with Thomas Tait.

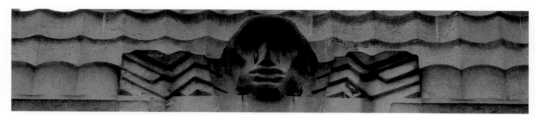

This page:
Top and center:
Daily Telegraph
newspaper building.
Two Portland stone bosses,
'Past', and 'Future', above
upper floor windows of
the zoned-back
120-foot-high building.
Sculptor:
Samuel Rabinovitch.

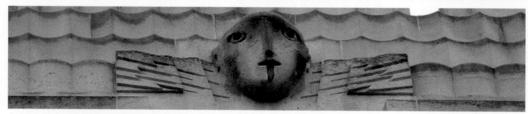

Below:
Daily Telegraph
newspaper building.
Relief of twin 'Mercuries',
over the main entrance.
Sculptor: A. Oakley.

Opposite:
Daily Telegraph
newspaper building.
Gilded metal grille
above the entrance doors.

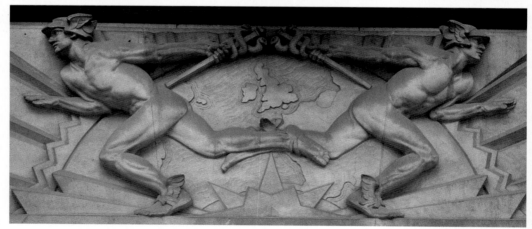

34

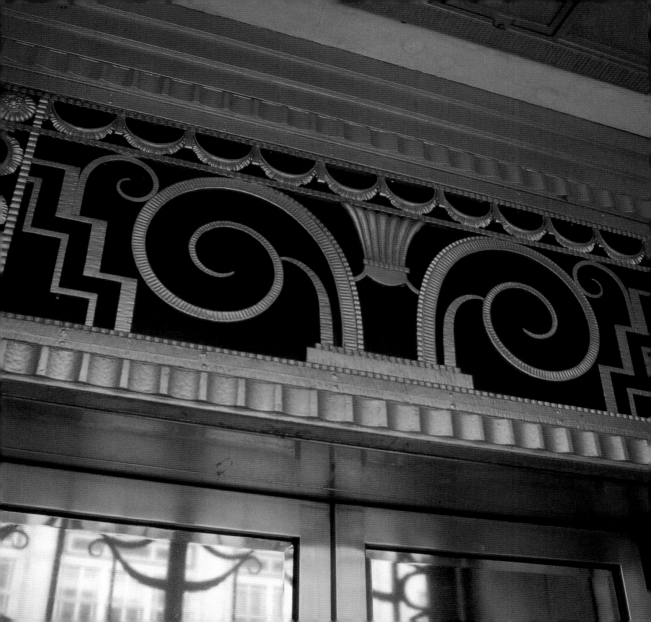

Daily Express newspaper
offices and printing
plant.
*Black vitrolite
and glass façade.*
Architects:
Sir Owen Williams,
with Ellis, Clarke.

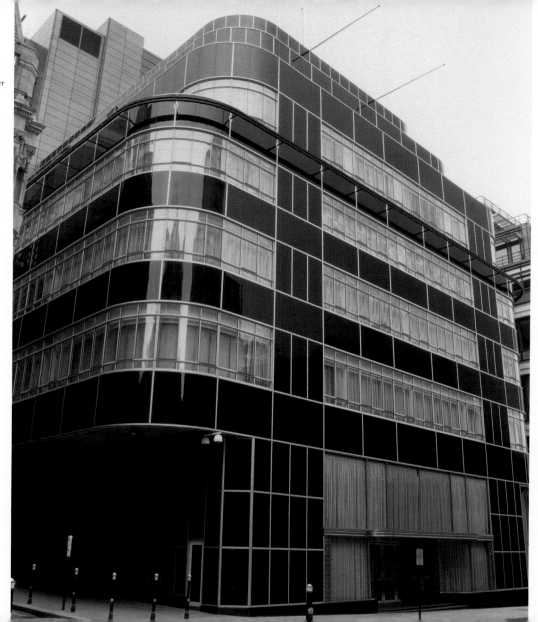

36

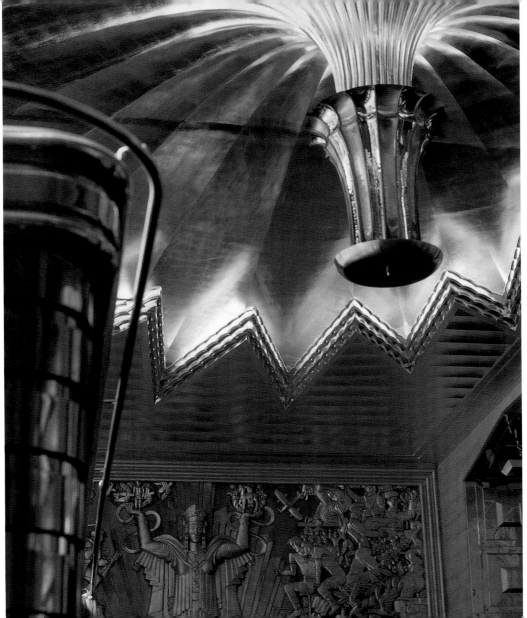

Daily Express newspaper
offices and printing
plant,
1930–32.
(Now Goldman Sachs
International),
133 Fleet Street, EC4.
*Faceted stainless steel
surfaces in the Daily Express
entrance hall.
John Betjeman said of
Atkinson's design
'... a fabulous Art Deco
entrance hall, with
wonderful rippling
confections of metal'.*
Interior design:
Robert F. Atkinson.

37

Daily Express newspaper offices and printing plant. *'Empire', one of two metal relief panels on opposite sides of the newspaper's entrance hall celebrate Lord Beaverbrook's Empire Free Trade campaign. The blue and black wavy-lined hard rubber floor represents the seas separating Great Britain from her Empire.* Sculptor: Eric Aumonier.

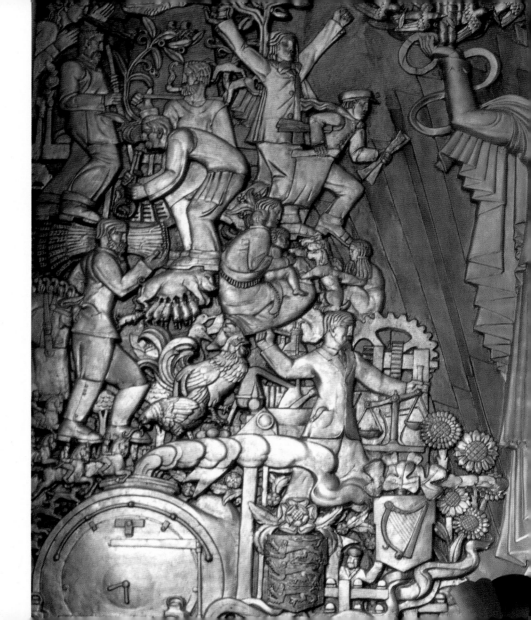

38

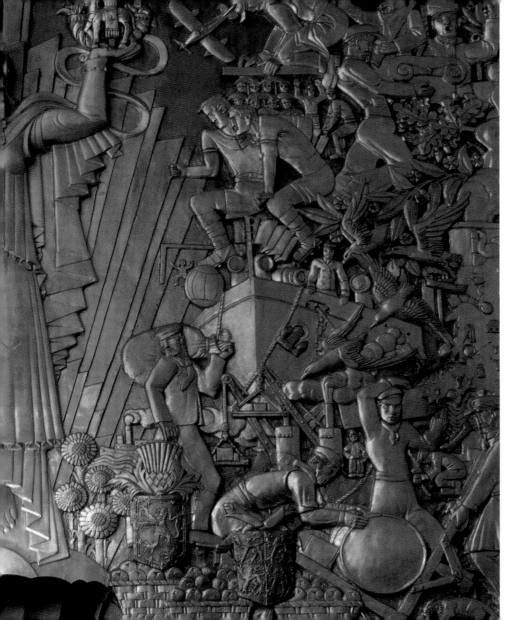

Among other works by
Eric Aumonier
are his archer at
East Finchley Underground
Station (page 106);
Broadway House, St. James,
and the Fortnum & Mason
ornate clock, Piccadilly.
It is said that the sculptor
was also responsible for
creating the statuary flanking
the 'stairway to heaven' in
Powell and Pressburger's
1948 film, 'A Matter of
Life and Death'.

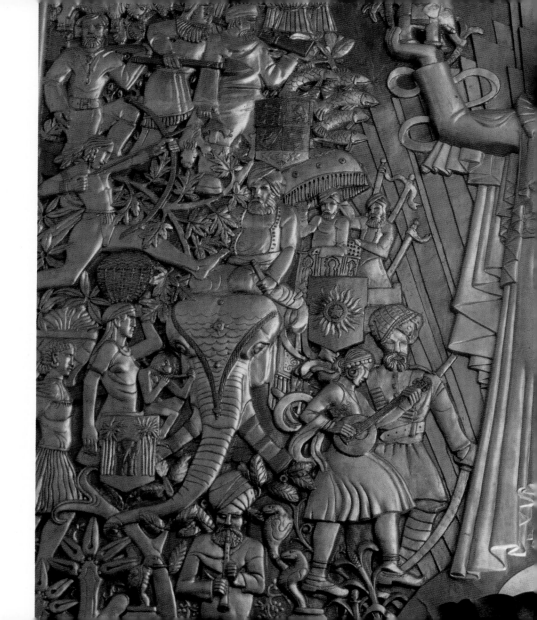

Daily Express newspaper
offices and printing plant.
*The second of the 'Empire'
relief panels in the
Daily Express entrance hall.*

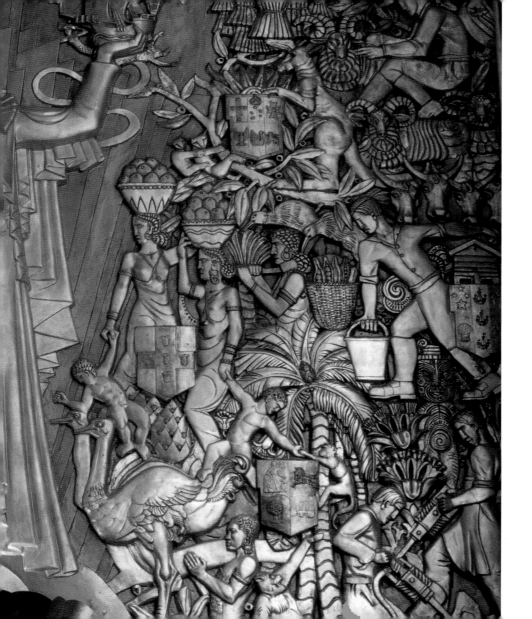

Serge Chermayeff, in the July 1932 Architectural Review, described Atkinson's entrance hall as 'a mass of fibrous plaster, gilded and silvered in the tinsel manner, suggesting a provincial picture palace'.

41

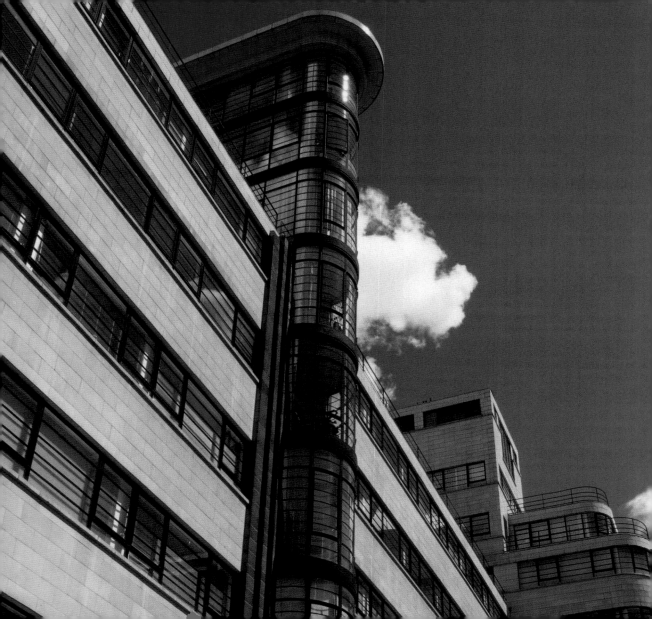

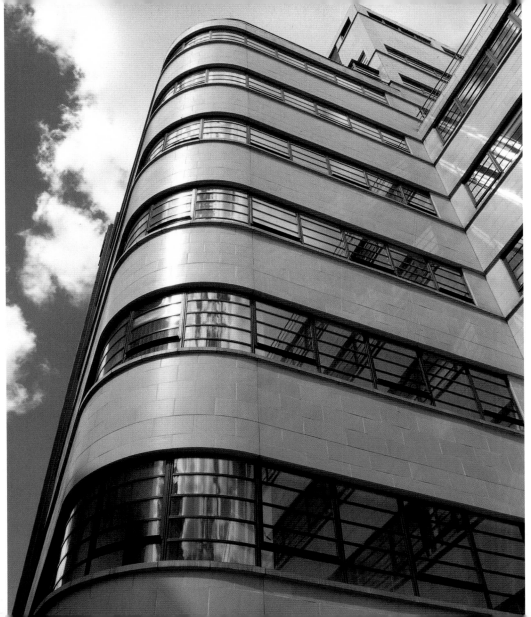

Opposite and this page:
Ibex House, 1937.
42–47 Minories, EC3.
The nine storey Ibex House,
clad in beige faïence, has
the longest strip windows
in London, and its curved
walls were inspired by
Erich Mendelsohn's
Berlin Schocken
department store.
Architects:
Fuller, Hall and Foulsham.

43

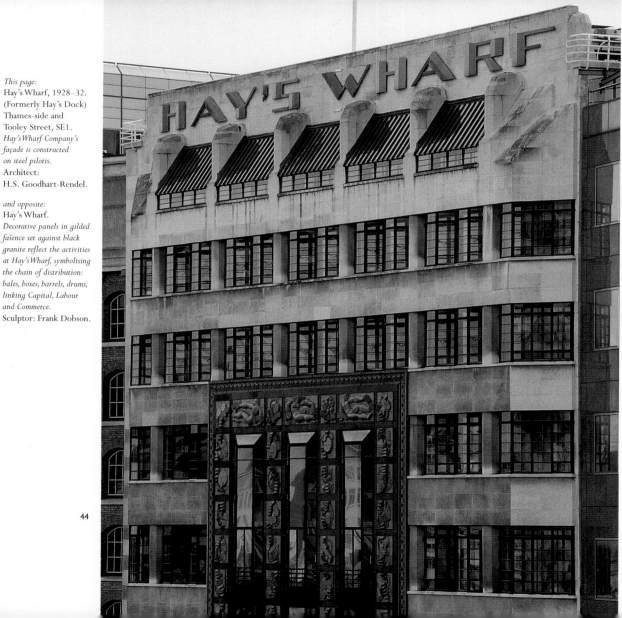

This page:
Hay's Wharf, 1928–32.
(Formerly Hay's Dock)
Thames-side and
Tooley Street, SE1.
*Hay's Wharf Company's
façade is constructed
on steel pilotis.*
Architect:
H.S. Goodhart-Rendel.

and opposite:
Hay's Wharf.
*Decorative panels in gilded
faïence set against black
granite reflect the activities
at Hay's Wharf, symbolising
the chain of distribution:
bales, boxes, barrels, drums,
linking Capital, Labour
and Commerce.*
Sculptor: Frank Dobson.

44

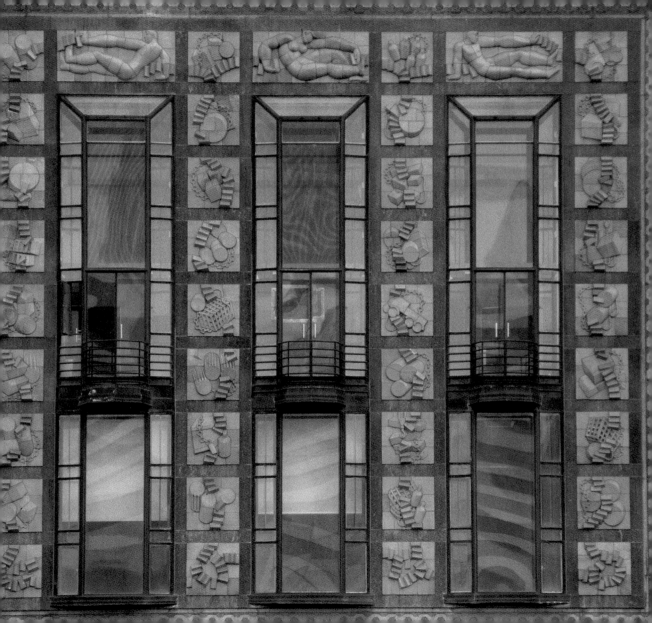

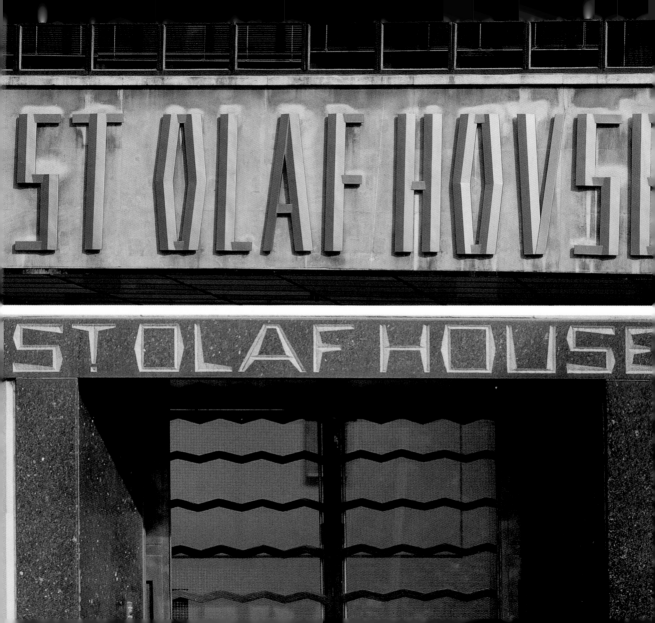

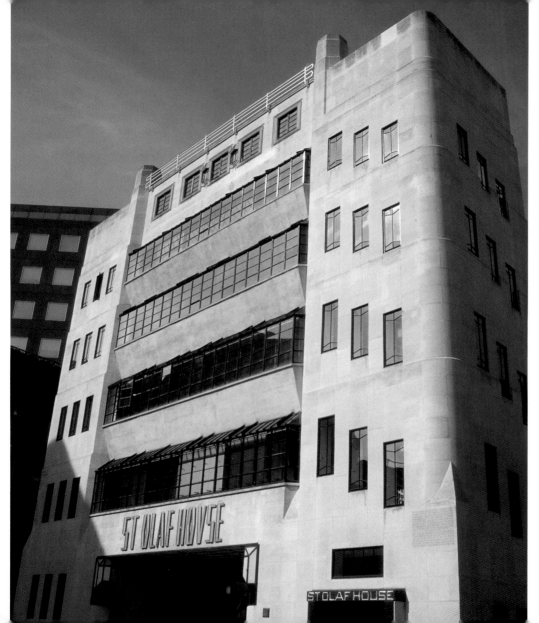

This page:
St. Olaf House,
1928–32.
Tooley Street, SE1.
*The curved Portland stone
building, St. Olaf House,
is the rear entrance of
the Thames-side
Hay's Wharf Company.*
Architects:
H.S. Goodhart-Rendel.

Opposite:
St. Olaf House.
Dimensional signage.
Designer:
Frank Dobson.

47

Department Stores & Shops

Barkers
department store,
1937–1938.
Kensington High Street,
W8.
*One of two bronze
and glass towers.*
Architect:
Bernard George.

'A NATION OF SHOPKEEPERS' is how Adam Smith, the 18th century Scottish economist characterised the English. London can still boast the existence of shops that were established in the 17th century. In the Twenties and Thirties department stores flourished in London, with names such as Army & Navy, Debenham & Freebody, Derry & Toms, Marshall & Snelgrove, Swan & Edgar and Waring & Gillow. Although some of these buildings still stand, the partnerships no longer exist.

When Gordon Selfridge built his Oxford Street emporium he employed the finest artisans, including Edgar Brandt and Gilbert Bayes.

The neighbouring department stores of Barkers' and Derry & Toms in High Street Kensington, both designed by Bernard George, emulate the Jazz Modern style of Paris in the late Twenties. Derry & Toms, with its ornate metal-work grilles, bas-reliefs and decorative cast aluminium relief panels by Walter Gilbert, and Barkers glass twin towers with spandrels displaying many of the store's products and gilded intaglio reliefs of chic ladies, still survive.

The International style influence is most evident in that of architect Joseph Emberton's Simpsons of Piccadilly men's store, and W. Crabtree with Slater, Moberley and C.H. Reilly's Peter Jones store with its curtain of glass exterior, are both reminiscent of Erich Mendelsohn's Schocken stores in Germany.

48

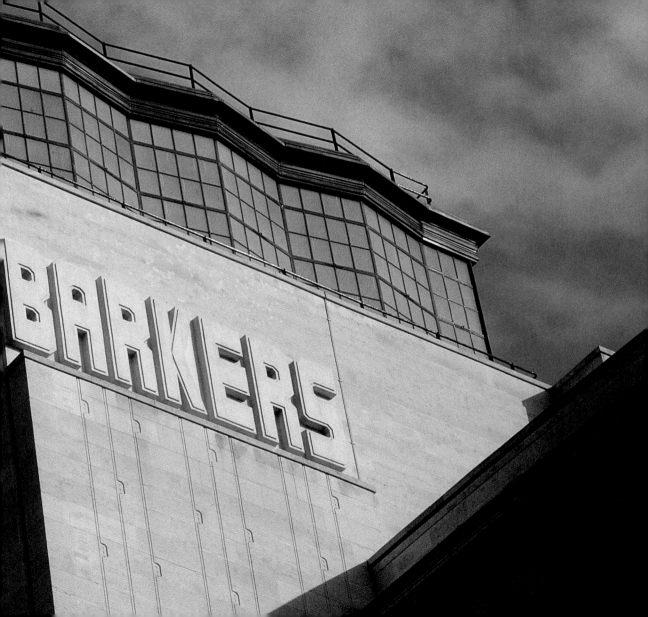

Barkers
department store.
Bronze spandrels depicting
store products include
cricket pads and stumps,
an armchair, a pair
of gloves, and a selection
of ladies shoes.

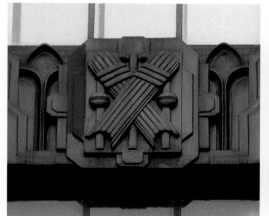
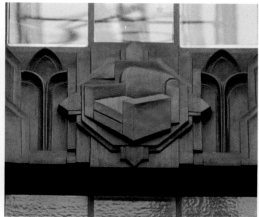
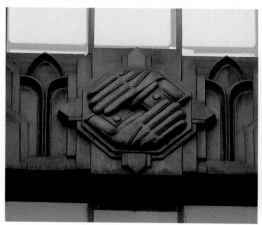
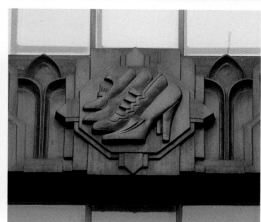

50

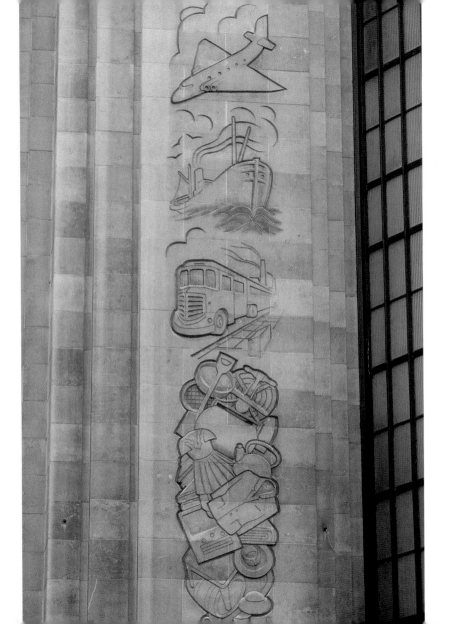

Barkers
department store.
*Included in this 1938
low-relief montage on one
of the twin glass towers
is a futuristic Vee-wing
jet engine aircraft.
The other panels include
images of an airship,
Oliver Vaughan
Snell Bulleid's 1937
LMS Pacific locomotive,
plus an array of
household goods.*

This page and opposite:
Barkers
department store.
Gilded intaglio plaques
of elegant ladies.

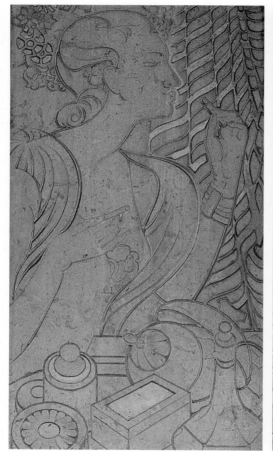

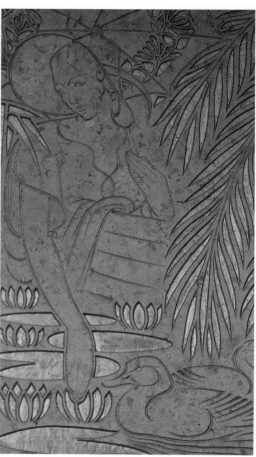

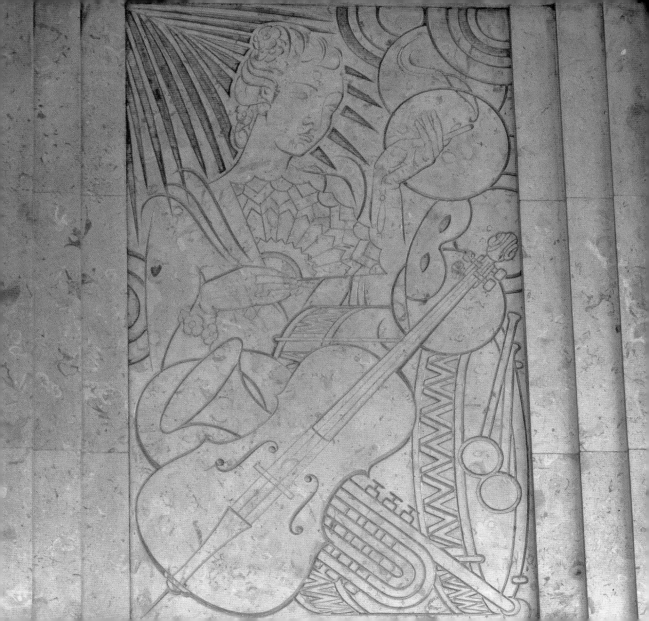

Derry & Toms
department store, 1933.
(Now British
Home Stores and
Marks & Spencer)
Kensington High Street,
W8.
*Cast and painted
aluminium frieze panel.*
Sculptor: Walter Gilbert.
Produced by the
Bromsgrove Guild.
Architect:
Bernard George.

*A one and a half acre
roof garden, that even
included live flamingoes,
was added in 1936-38.
It is still in use to this day.*

54

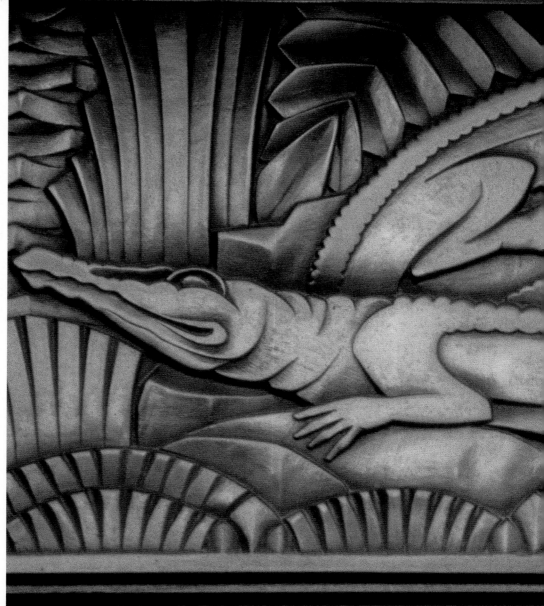

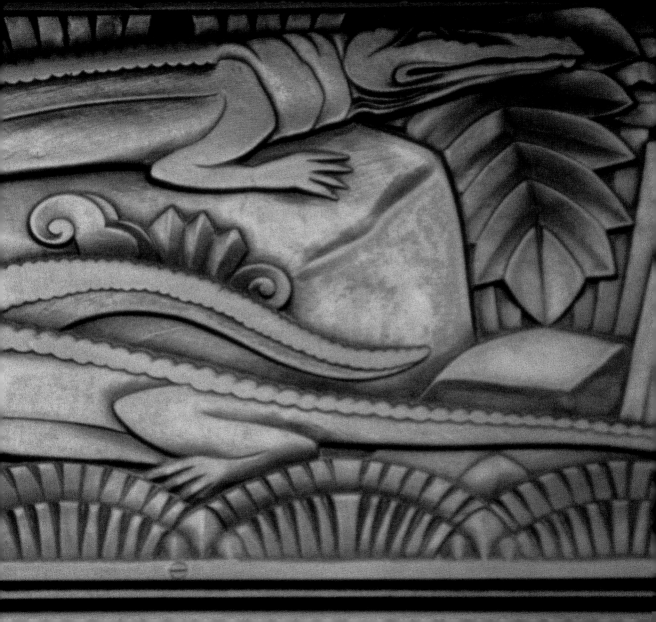

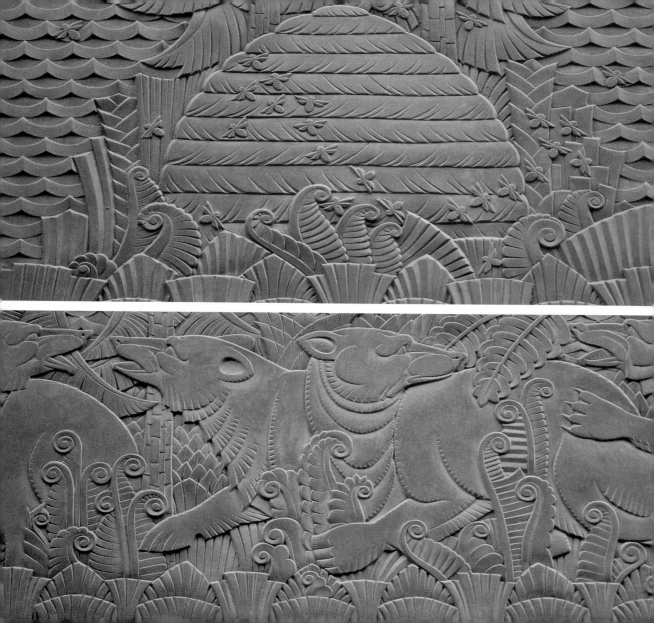

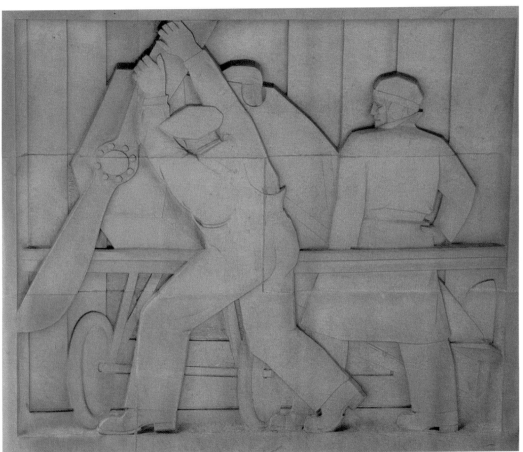

This page and opposite:
Simpson Piccadilly
menswear store, 1936.
(Now Waterstone's)
202 Piccadilly, W1.
Neon and metal signage.
Architects:
Joseph Emberton,
Felix Samuely and
László Maholy-Nagy.
Logotype designers for
Simpson and DAKS:
Eric Gill and
Ashley Havinden.

Joseph Emberton was
also the designer of the
Olympia Exhibition Hall
and Dorset House
apartment building,
as well as the kiosks for
Abdulla Cigarettes and
Mackintosh's Toffee
at the British Empire
Exhibition, Wembley, 1924.

Eric Gill was also
commissioned to design
the signage for the
Army & Navy Stores Ltd,
(1929)
and W.H. Smith (1903).

Ashley Havinden
was the art director
of WS Crawford Ltd
advertising agency.

58

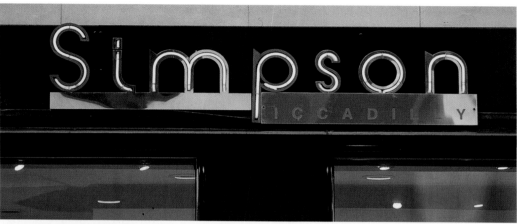

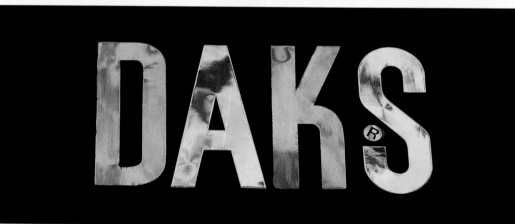

Simpson

PICCADILLY

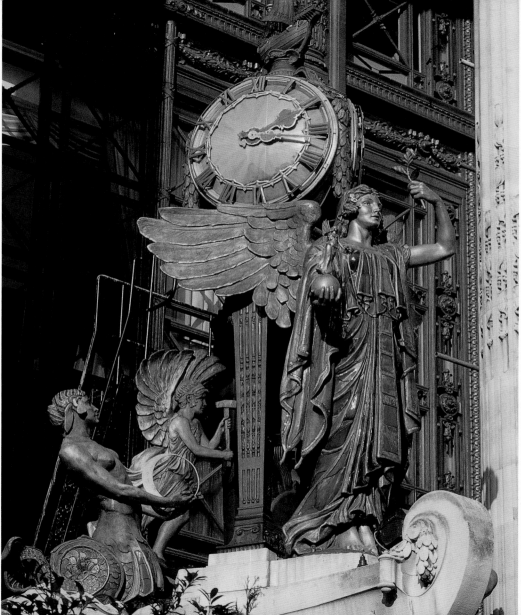

This page:
Selfridges department
store, 1907–28.
400 Oxford Street, W1.
*The ornamental 11-foot high
'Queen of Time', c.1925,
stands as a sentinel above the
entrance of one of London's
largest department stores.*
Sculptor:
Gilbert William Bayes, RA.
Architects:
Robert F. Atkinson
with Daniel Burnham,
supervised by
Sir John Burnet.

Opposite:
Selfridges
department store.
*Brass commemorative
floor medallion at the
main entrance.*
Sculptor:
Gilbert William Bayes, RA.

*The store's lacquer and metal
on wood lift cage door panels,
'Les cigognes d'Alsace'
(Storks of Alsace)
by French designer
Edgar Brandt, 1928.
A complete lift cage and doors
are on display at the
Museum of London. Other
examples are housed in the
Victoria & Albert Museum
and the Brighton Museum.*

60

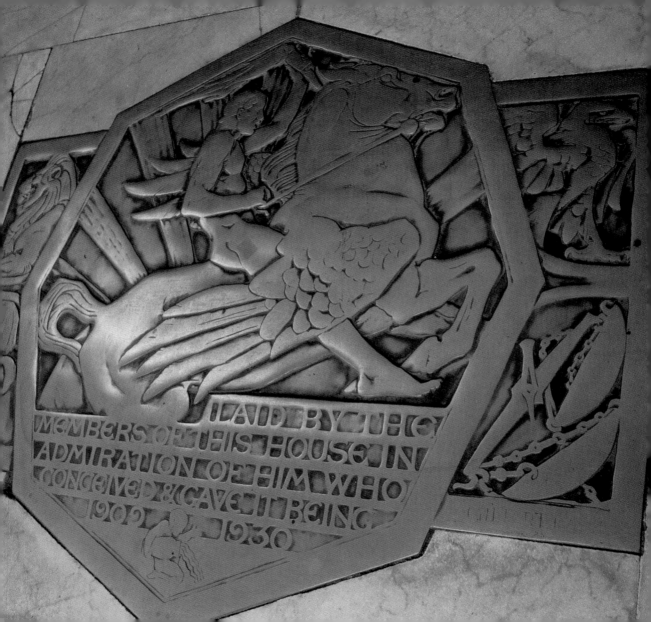

LAID BY THE
MEMBERS OF THIS HOUSE IN
ADMIRATION OF HIM WHO
CONCEIVED & GAVE IT BEING
1909 — 1930

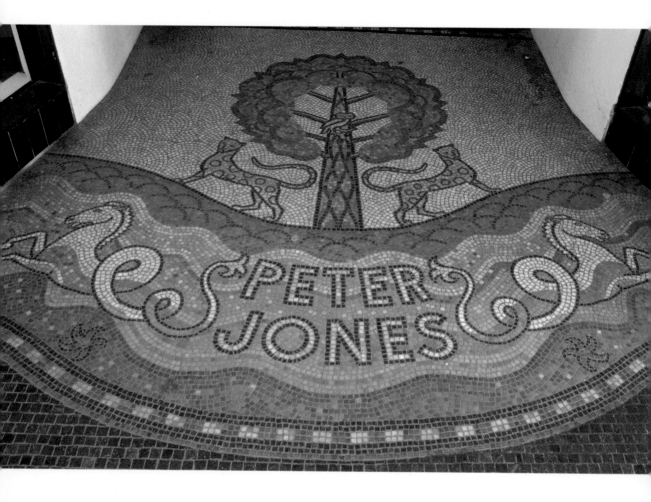

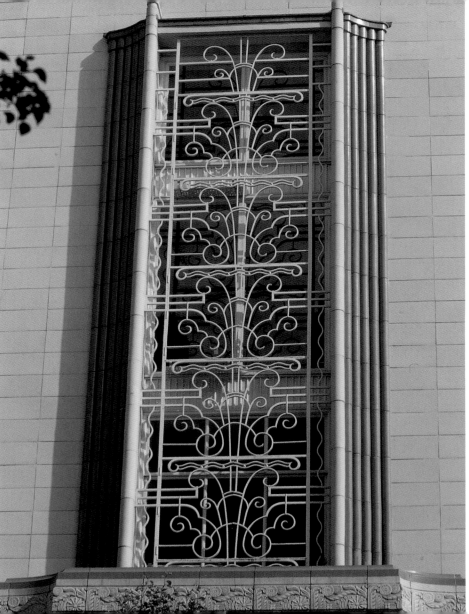

This page:
Lilley & Skinner
footwear manufacturers
(Now retail store)
368 Oxford Street, W1.
Window grille.

Opposite:
Peter Jones department
store, 1936–38.
Sloane Square, SWI.
Mosaic floor at the
Cadogan Gardens
side entrance.
Architects:
W. Crabtree with
Slater, Moberley and
C.H. Reilly (Consultant).

Above:
Gandolfi
ballet shoemakers,
1949.
150 Marylebone Road,
NW1.

Below:
T. Fox & Co. Ltd,
c.1935.
Umbrella and walking
stick manufacturers.
118 London Wall, EC2.
Black vitrolite façade by
Pilkington Brothers, and
shopfitting by Pollards.

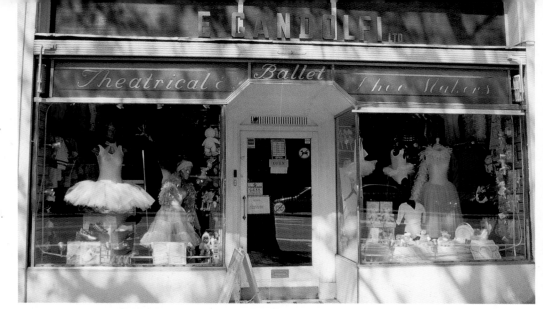

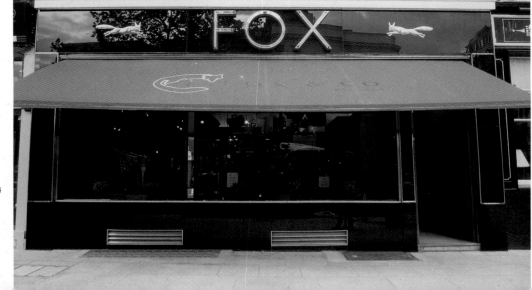

64

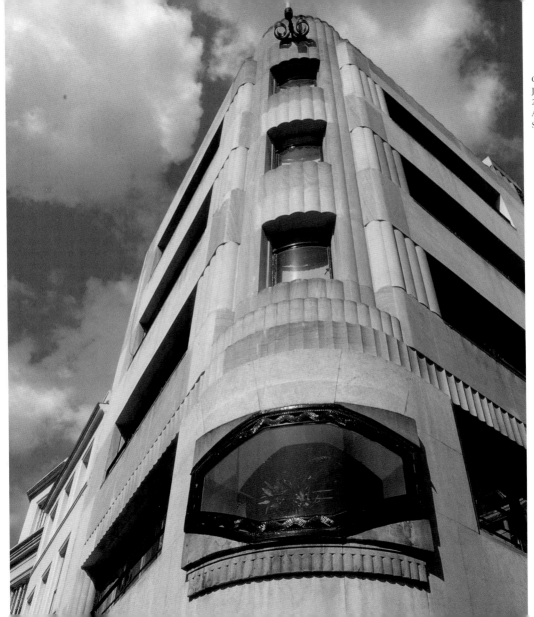

Greybrook House,
Joseph retail store, 1929.
28 Brook Street, W1.
Architect:
Sir John Burnet & Partners.

Hotels

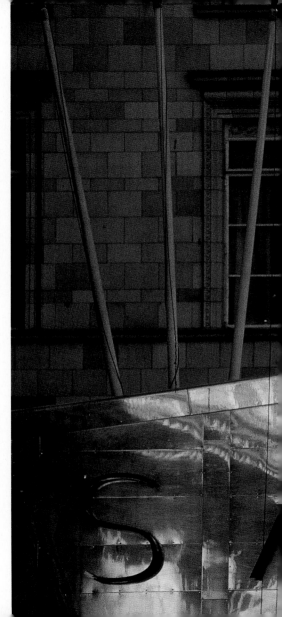

The Savoy, 1889.
Strand, WC1.
*The hotel was built on
the former site of the
13th century Savoy Palace.
The stainless steel canopy,
designed by architects
Easton and Robertson,
was added over the Strand
entrance during the
hotel's redecoration by
Basil Ionides, 1926–29.
The canopy, surmounted by
Frank Lynn Jenkins's
statue of Count Peter,
has been likened to
the Rolls Royce
'Spirit of Ecstasy'
radiator and mascot.
The Savoy Hotel closed in
December 2007 for extensive
renovations and reopened in
October 2010.*

'THE GREAT ADVANTAGE OF A HOTEL is that it's a refuge from home life'. – George Bernard Shaw. When Richard D'Oyly Carte built his Savoy Theatre in 1881 to stage the Gilbert and Sullivan operettas, his experience of receiving great service while travelling in the U.S. inspired him to create a hostelry where he could provide his patrons with luxurious comfort, and he opened The Savoy in 1889. Ever striving for excellence, in 1929 the Savoy commissioned Basil Ionides to remodel a number of public areas and suites in the hotel, and to redesign the adjoining Savoy Theatre, which in 1990 tragically was gutted by fire, but has since been lovingly restored based on sketches and plans housed in the Victoria & Albert Museum's archives.

Ionides also redecorated the Savoy's then-sister hotel, Claridge's, in 1929. That year, in an interview with *Studio Magazine*, Ionides stated: 'Simplicity is of course the note to be aimed at today; and also good colours. The day of the elaborate plaster ceiling is gone and its place is taken by simple stepping or coffering.'

Opposite The Savoy is architect Oliver Bernard's Strand Palace Hotel, its razzle-dazzle lobby with its illuminated panels of fluted plate glass (now in the V&A Museum) is revered as an icon of Moderne design. Another Art Deco treasure is Piccadilly's Park Lane Hotel's lobby and ballroom, with spectacular murals, gilded balustrades and cylindrical stair lights.

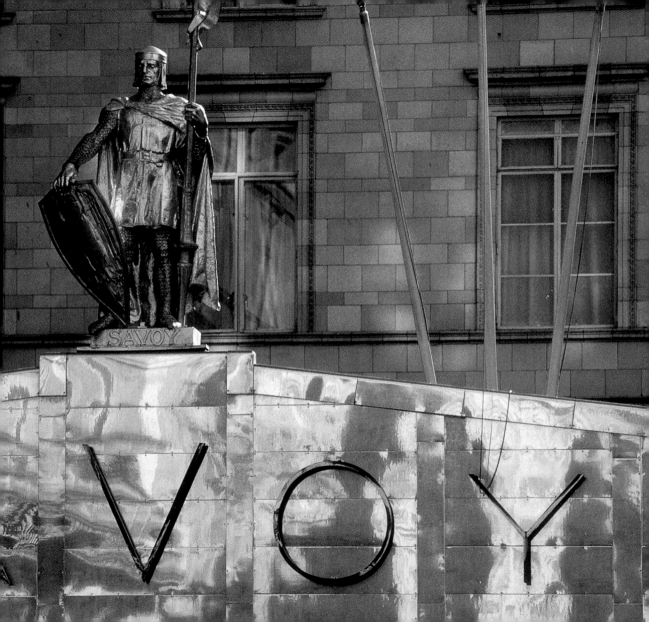

Claridge's.
(Formerly part of
the Savoy Group).
55 Brook Street, W1.
*Zigzag design mirror,
and wall light fittings
in the hotel lobby.*
Refurbished by
Basil Ionides in 1929,
and by Oswald Milne
in 1929–30.

68

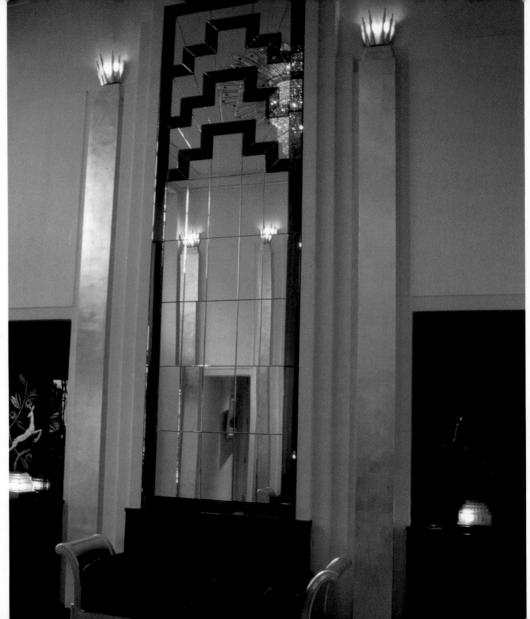

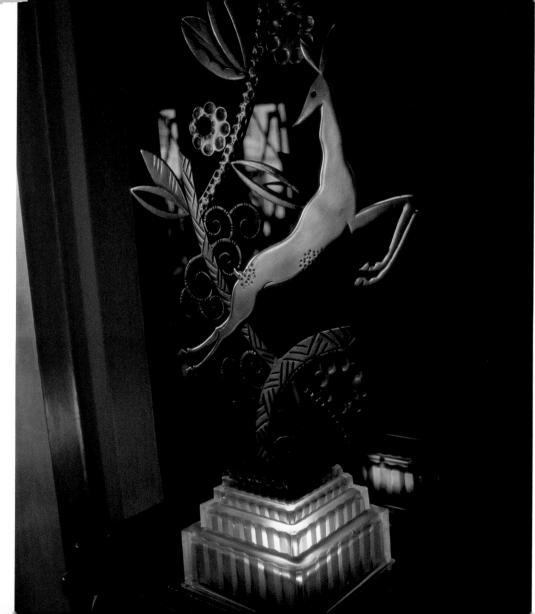

Claridge's.
*A Lalique glass lamp
decorated with a
leaping deer and foliage
in the hotel's lobby.*

This page:
Claridge's.
Brook Suite mantel clock.

Opposite:
Claridge's.
Brook Suite.

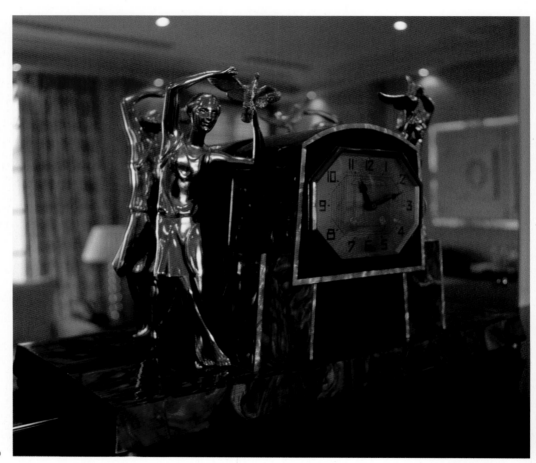

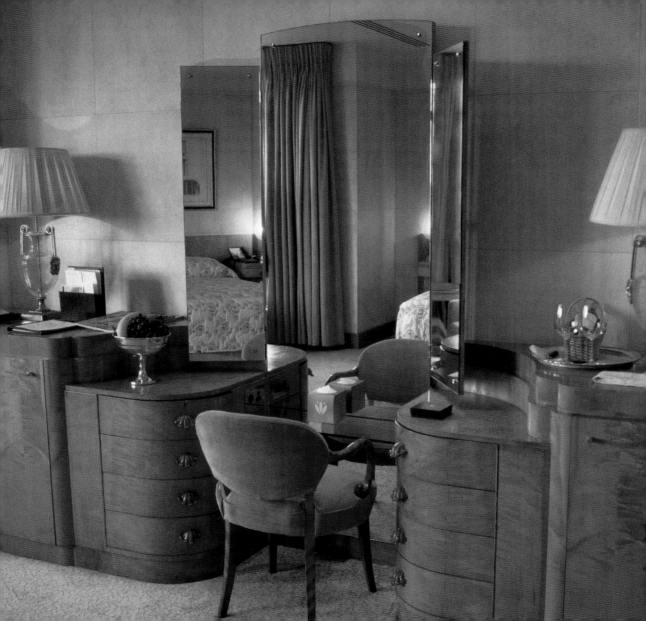

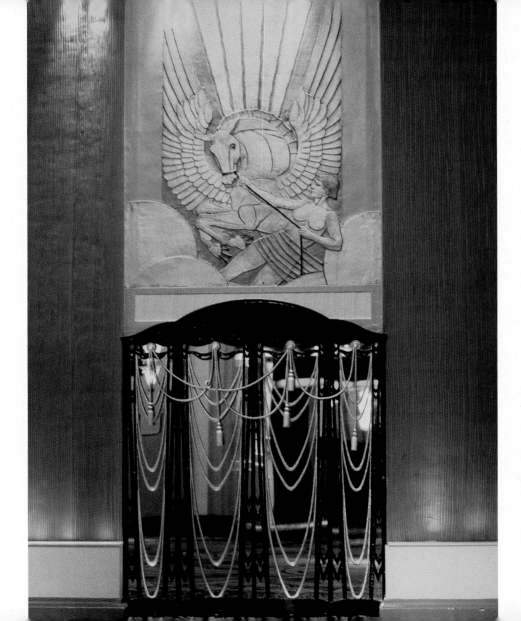

This page:
Park Lane Hotel, 1927.
Piccadilly, W1.
*One of several gilded
bas-reliefs above the
Ballroom doors.*
Designer: Kenneth Anns.
Architect: Henry Tanner.

Opposite:
Park Lane Hotel.
*Mural in the lobby
of the hotel.*

72

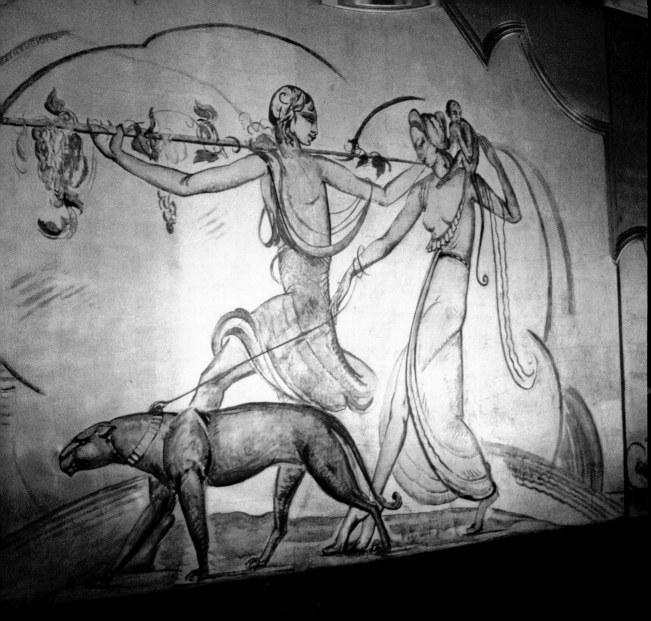

This page:
Park Lane Hotel.
Mirror and side table
surmounted by light fitting.

Opposite:
Park Lane Hotel.
Illuminated glass and
gold metal balustrade.

74

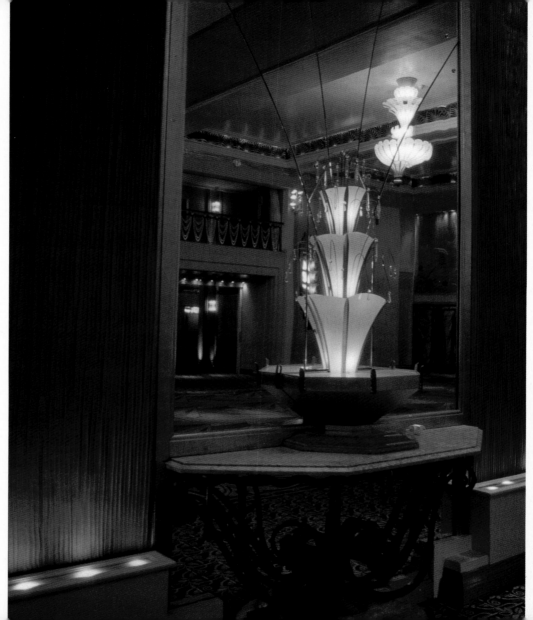

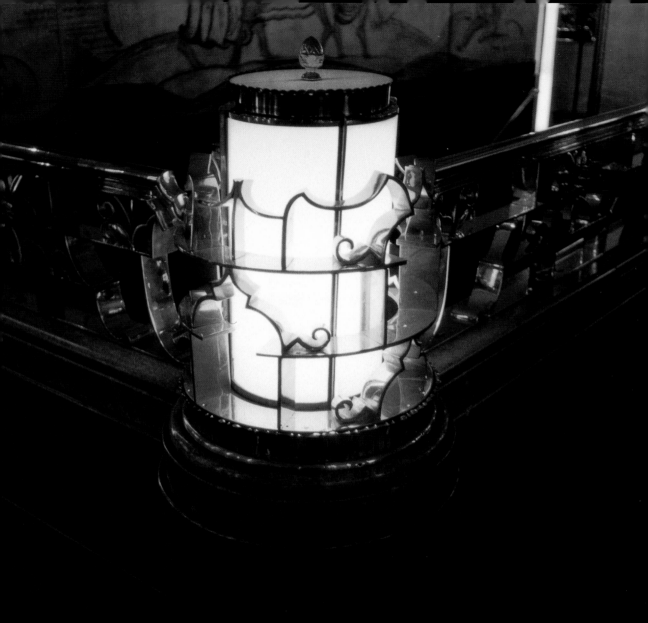

Top and below:
Lyons Oxford Corner House, 1920s.
(On the former site of the Oxford Music Hall)
14–16 Oxford Street, W1.
Two decorative grilles.
Architect:
Oliver Percy Bernard.

In 2011 the building was renovated for retail development.

Oliver Bernard, the architect of hotels and restaurants for the J. Lyons Group, also designed the J. Lyons Middle Eastern-themed restaurant at the 1924 Empire Exhibition at Wembley.

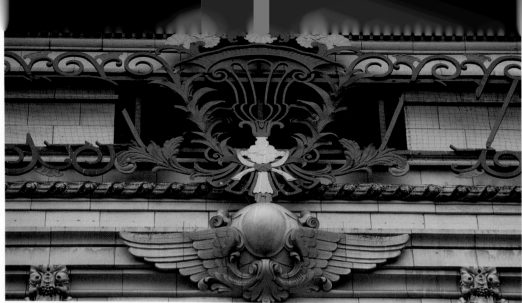

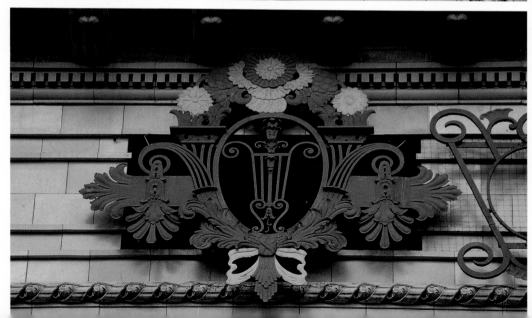

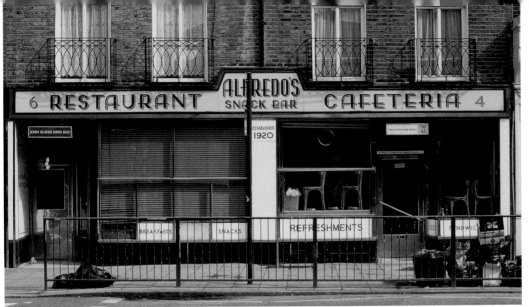

Above:
Alfredo's Cafe, 1920s.
(Now S & M
Sausage & Mash Cafe)
4–6 Essex Road, N1.
*Chrome, cream vitrolite
and Formica façade.*

Below:
Pellicci's Cafe, 1920s.
332 Bethnal Green
Road, E2.
*Chrome, cream vitrolite,
leaded glass
and Formica façade.
Interior marquetry panels
by Achille Capocci, 1946.
Both cafes were
frequented by the
infamous Kray Brothers.*

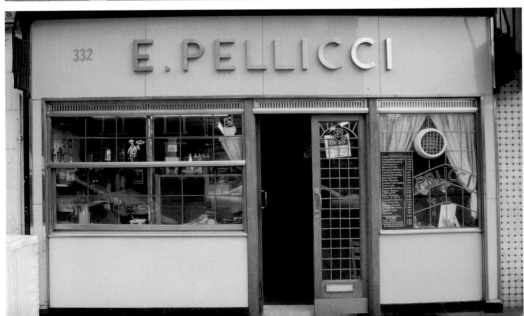

Cinemas, Theatres & Sport

Gaumont Palace, 1934,
(Now Habitat Store)
39 King's Road, SW3.
Film pioneer
William Friese-Greene,
on one of three ceramic
plaques (page 90)
on the façade of the
former cinema built on
the site of Friese-Greene's
laboratory and studio.
Sculptor:
Newbury A. Trent.
Architects:
William E. Trent and
Ernest F. Tully.

Like the Gaumont Palace,
the Neo-Egyptian-style
New Gallery Cinema
(1925), was converted
in 2006 into the
Habitat Regent Street store.
121-123 Regent Street, W1.

'I WANT TO RING LONDON WITH ODEONS!' declared Oscar Deutsch, whose Odeon circuit of cinemas dominated London and its suburbs. His flagship, the 2116-seat Odeon Leicester Square (1937), with its 120-foot tower made of polished granite, was originally planned to be clad in yellow faïence tiles. Its interior is flanked by leaping gilded figures by Raymond Britton Reviere, and sports fake leopard-skin covered seats, and a Compton organ that rippled with coloured lights. Other notable London Odeons are those of Barnet (1935) designed by Edgar Simmons, and Erith (1938), Isleworth (1935), Muswell Hill (1936) and Woolwich (1937) designed by George Coles.

The advent of talkies in 1927 brought about a boom in new cinema construction and by 1932, London had over 250 cinemas. The lyrics from the 1930 song 'Knocking Down London' included the line '…There ain't no money in an Adams house, but there's oodles in an Odeon…'

Cinemas with resplendent names such as Regal, Regent, Rex, Ritz and Roxy were ubiquitous throughout the capital.

'*Say Gren-AH-dah*'. Another chain of cinemas was Sidney Bernstein's Granada, his flagship being the Granada Tooting (1931), its fantasy interior resembling a Gothic cathedral, as was the Granada Woolwich (1937), which was billed as 'the most romantic theatre ever built' (both now bingo halls). Many of the Granada interiors were designed by Russian-born Theodore Komisarjesky. Sadly, the increased popularity of television in the 1960s signalled the death-knell of the super-cinema.

'*The last remaining seats…*' Of the Granada chain in London alone, twelve were demolished, eleven ('legs eleven') turned into bingo halls, five into supermarkets, one became a McDonald's, and the rest were turned into storage facilities, car showrooms, fitness clubs, training centres, and wrestling halls. Only six still operate as cinemas.

What would the British film pioneer William Friese-Greene have made of all this, who had tragically dropped dead after giving an impassioned speech at a film exhibitors and renters meeting. The poverty-stricken Greene ironically was found to have just one shilling and sixpence in his pocket, the price of a cinema ticket. A lavish funeral was arranged by a shame-faced industry. The floral tribute atop his hearse was a film projector and a screen with the simple epitaph 'THE END'.

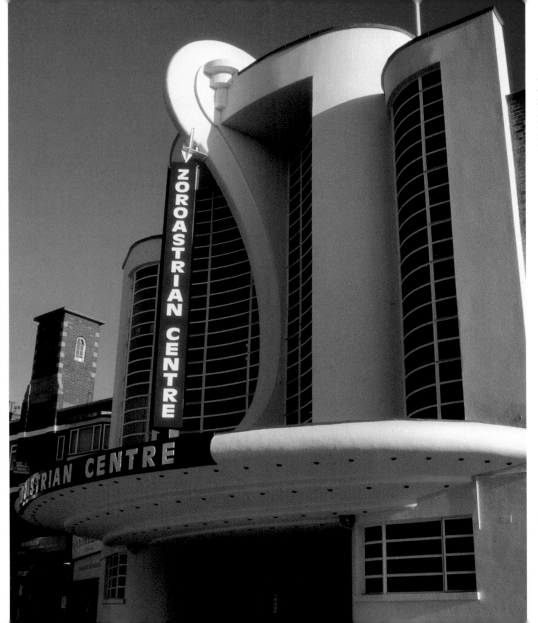

Grosvenor Rayners Lane Cinema, 1936. (Now a Zoroastrian Centre) Alexandra Avenue, Rayners Lane, Harrow. Architect: Frederick E. Bromige.

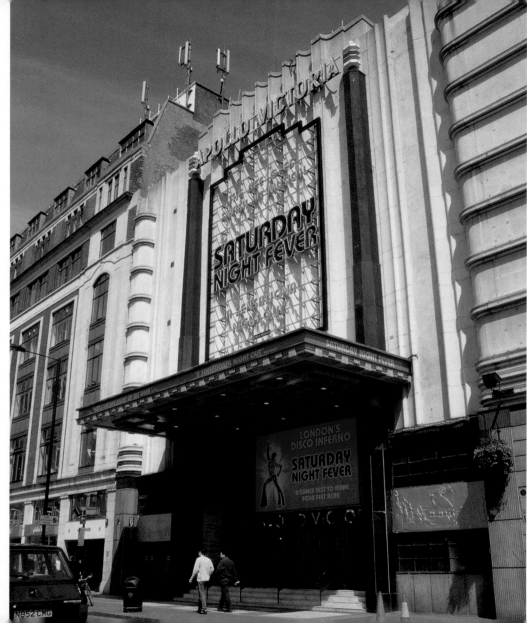

This page:
New Victoria Cinema,
1928–30.
(Now Apollo Victoria)
Wilton Road and
Vauxhall Bridge Road,
SW1.
The Apollo Victoria is
faced in slabs of cast
Portland stone.
Architects:
Ernest Warmsley Lewis
and William E. Trent.

Opposite:
Apollo Victoria.
Exit sign, cast grey
granite ventilation grille.

80

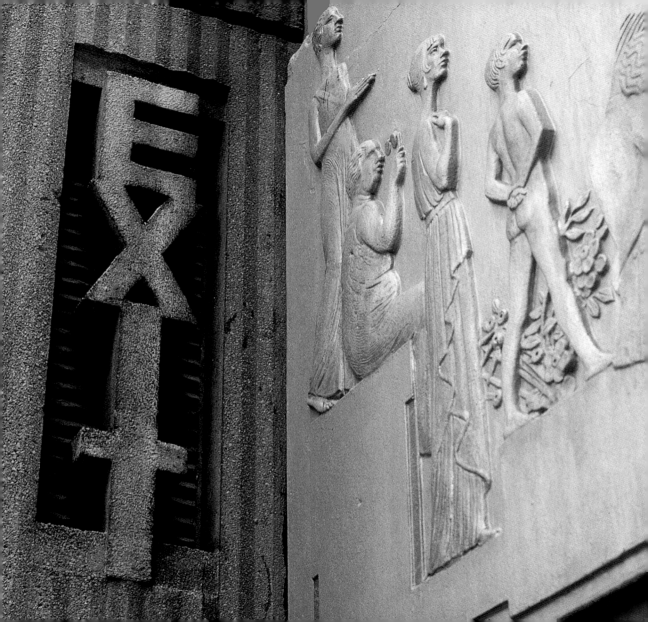

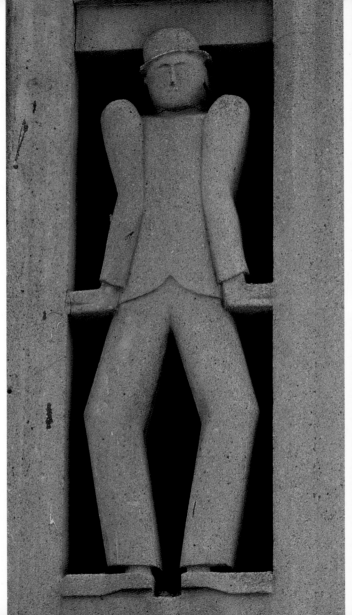

This page:
Apollo Victoria.
Figure of Charlie Chaplin cast grey granite ventilation grille.

and opposite:
Apollo Victoria.
Two silvered bas-relief panels in the lap process depicting two distinct film genres, on the exterior above either side of the exit doors.
Sculptor:
Newbury A. Trent (brother of one of the building's architect, William E. Trent).

Architect Ernest Warmsley Lewis described his plan for the cinema to be a 'mermaid's palace'.

82

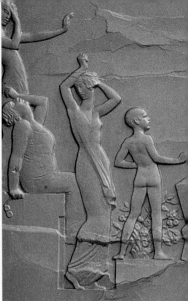

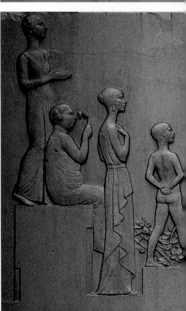

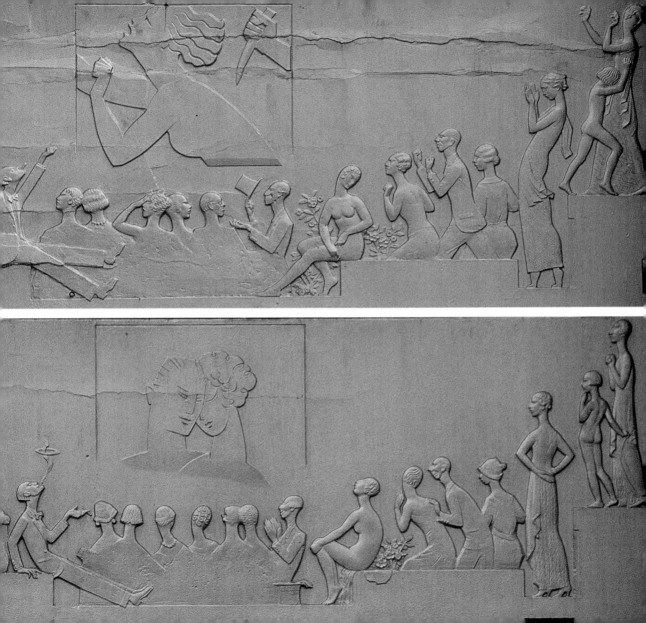

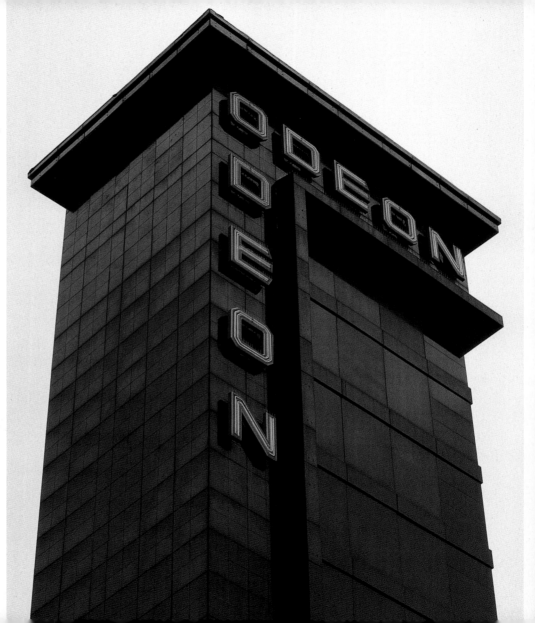

This page:
Odeon Leicester Square
Cinema, 1937.
(On the former site of
the Alhambra Music Hall)
Leicester Square, WC2.
90-foot-high tower in
black polished granite,
with neon lighting.
A landmine dropped in
1940 badly damaged the
Odeon Leicester Square's
foyer and its twelve etched
glass doors.
Architects:
Andrew Mather,
Harry Weedon and
Thomas Braddock.

Opposite:
Odeon Coronet Theatre,
1937.
(Now Gateway House)
John Wilson Street,
Woolwich, SE18.
Architect:
George Coles.

Across the road from the
Odeon Coronet stands
the Theodore Komisarjevsky
designed Granada Woolwich
(now a bingo hall),
its Gothic-style interior
echoes Montreal's
Notre-Dame Basilica.

84

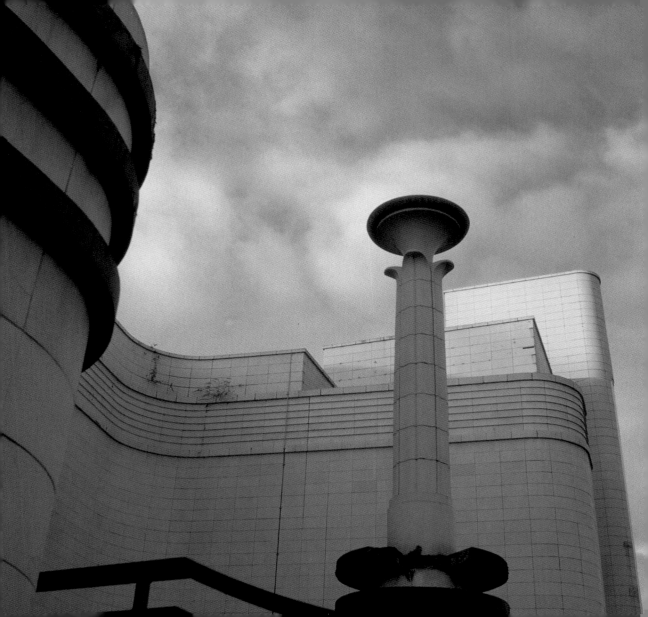

Top:
Carlton Cinema, 1930.
161–169 Essex Road,
N10.
*Façade with
Karnak-inspired
lotus-top columns.*
Architect:
George Coles.

Below:
Carlton Cinema.
*Egyptian-style
decorative tile panel.*

*Other Egyptian-style
cinemas in London include
the Kensington (1926);
the Carlton,
Upton Park (1929);
the Luxor, Twickenham
(1929); and the Astoria,
Streatham (1930).*

*The one-time Mecca
Bingo Hall was recently
purchased for use as
a church and cinema.*

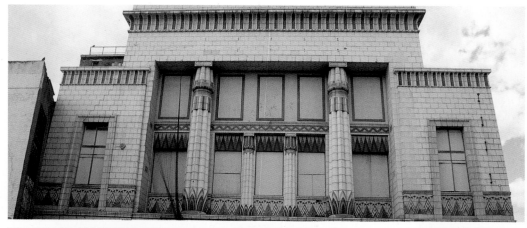

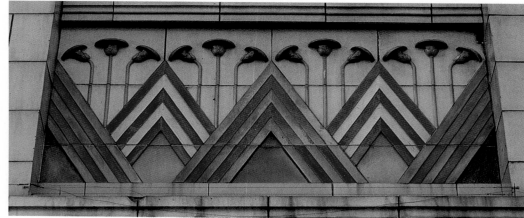

86

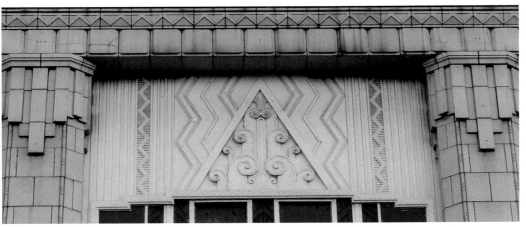

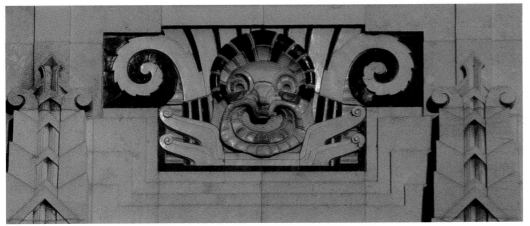

Top:
Troxy, 1933.
(Now a Mecca
Bingo Hall)
Commercial Road, E1.
*Cream faïence tiles of
the 3,520-seat cinema.*
Architect:
George Coles.

*'...The Troxy, another
elegant super-cinema,
was opened near Poplar
and charged sixpence.
It featured Vandamm's
twelve-piece orchestra and
an organist, who were
elevated onto the stage
during intervals. There was a
three-hour film programme,
including three top
variety acts.'*
Excerpt from
the memoirs of
David Schwartzman
(the author's father).

Below:
Odeon Richmond Hill,
1929.
Richmond-upon-Thames.
*Egyptian-Aztec
style decoration.*
Architects:
Leathart & Granger.

This page and opposite:
Warner Theatre, 1938.
(On the former site
of Daly's Theatre).
Cranbourne Street and
Leicester Square, WC2.
*Two cream-coloured
marble panels representing
the spirits of Sight and
Sound are placed either
side of a tower carrying
the Warner name.*
Sculptor:
Bainbridge Copnall.
Architects:
Edward A. Stone and
T. R. Somerford.

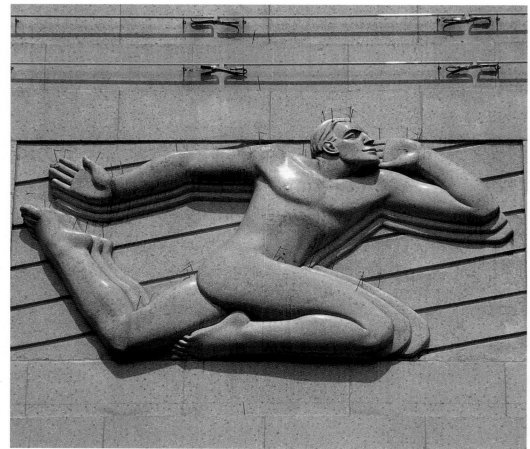

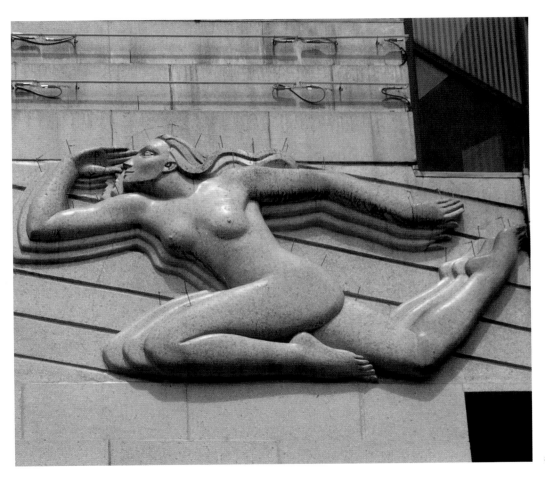

Left:
Whitehall Theatre, 1930.
(Now Trafalgar Studios,
built on the site of the
former Ship Tavern)
Whitehall, SW1.
Mask of Tragedy, exterior.
Architect:
Edward A. Stone.

Right:
Gaumont Palace, 1934.
(Now a Habitat store)
206 Kings Road, SW3.
*Ceramic decorative masks
of Comedy and Tragedy are
alongside the plaque of
William Friese-Greene
(page 78). There are also
two entry-panels:
'The Awakening of Science
to the Force of the Elements'
and 'The Harmony of the
Elements of Film'.*
Sculptor:
Newbury A. Trent.
Architects:
William E. Trent and
Ernest F. Tully.

Opposite:
Royal Academy of
Dramatic Arts (RADA),
1933.
62 Gower Street, WC1.
*Two figures supporting
masks of Tragedy and Comedy.*
Sculptor: Alan Durst.

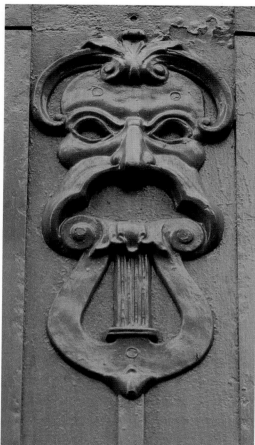

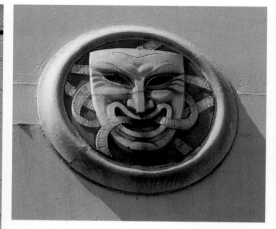

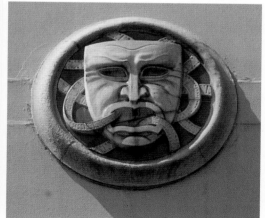

90

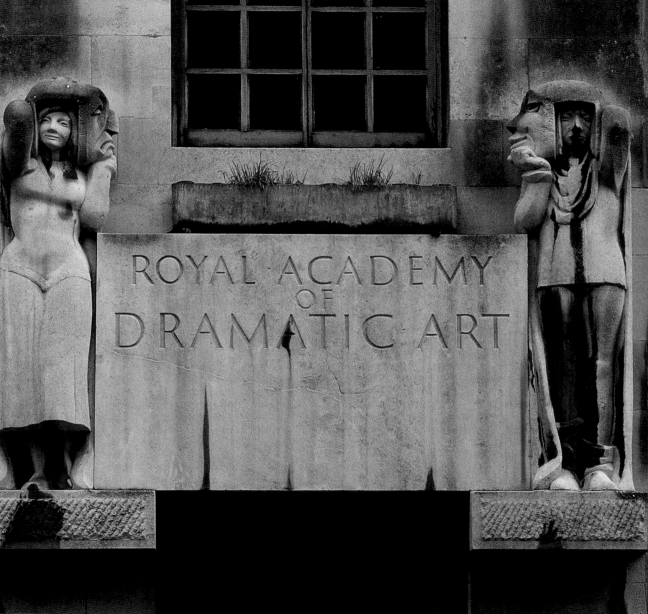

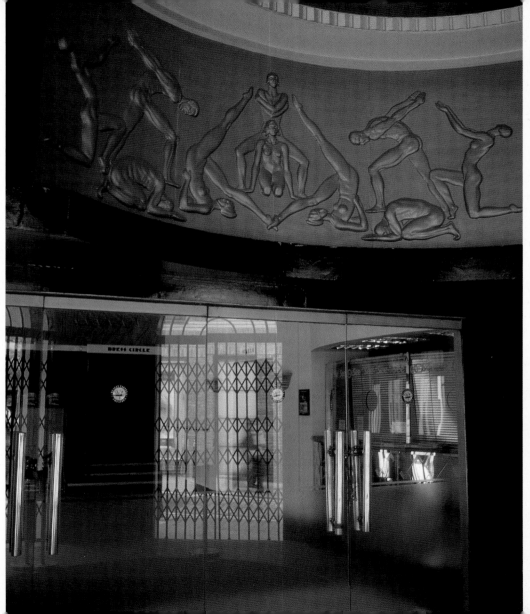

This page:
Cambridge Theatre, 1930.
Earlham Street,
Seven Dials, WC2.
Bas-relief panel, foyer.
Architects:
Wimperis, Simpson
and Guthrie.

Opposite above:
Two Portland stone friezes by
Gilbert William Bayes, R.A.:
Saville Theatre, 1931.
(Now Odeon
Covent Garden)
135 Shaftesbury Avenue,
W1.
The 'Romance of the
Twentieth Century' section
of the 130-foot long frieze,
'Drama through the Ages'
includes the characters
Sherlock Holmes and his
nemesis Moriarty, a chorus
line of Flappers, and a
couple of theatre patrons.
Architects:
T.B. Bennett and Son.

Below:
Lords Cricket Ground,
1934.
St. John's Wood Road and
Wellington Road, NW8.
A cricketer holds up
the small urn containing
the prized 'Ashes'.
Other figures represent
various sports.

92

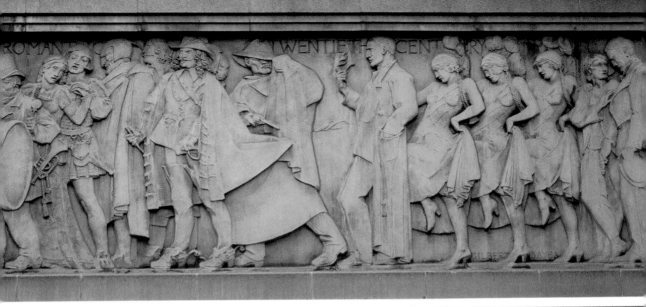

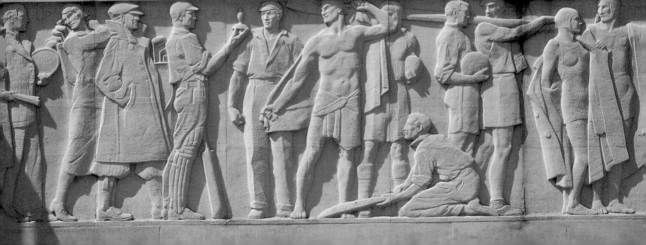

London Transport

'THE GREATEST PATRON OF THE ARTS who this century has so far produced in England...' is how German-born architectural historian Nikolaus Pevsner described Frank Pick.

Pick was the commercial manager of the London Electric Railway Company, with overall control of everything from the design of timetables to Underground Stations, and later became the Chief Executive Officer of the London Transport Passenger Board. In 1923 he began a long and successful collaboration with architect Charles Holden.

In 1927, Frank Pick brought together a motley crew consisting of a red-headed Quaker, Holden, a New York Jew, Jacob Epstein, and a self-styled 'married monk', Eric Gill, making Holden the sole architect responsible for designing Broadway House, the new London Transport headquarters at 55 Broadway, atop St. James Underground Station.

Holden's plan was to build a tower based on Athens' 'Tower of Winds'. The Portland stone cruciform building was to be decorated with sculptural pieces by Epstein, Gill, and the young Henry Moore, among others. Epstein, whose work was already plagued by controversy – having his Rima memorial tarred and feathered twice, was smuggled onto the site, where he and the other sculptors worked in situ. Epstein's two major pieces, 'Day' and 'Night', are above the east and north entrances, respectively. 'Night', being in constant shadow, was cut deeper than its companion piece. At its unveiling, the sculptor's graphic naked figures were characterised as obscene, prompting one LTPB director's offer to pay for the removal of the two offending pieces. Epstein was forced to trim one and a half inches off the private parts from 'Day'. These twin pieces went on to be regarded among the most important British public sculptures of the 20th century.

Holden was further given the responsibility of designing a large number of Underground stations on the Piccadilly line (1930–34) and its extension (1935–38), and the Northern line (1940–41).

Following a visit with Pick to the Netherlands and Germany, Holden, influenced by the red brick designs of Dutch architect Willem Marinus Dudok, built stations such as at Osterley, and his drum-like ticket halls for Southgate and Arnos Grove stations were said to have inspired Wells Coates' design of his classic round Echo AD65 bakelite radio of 1934.

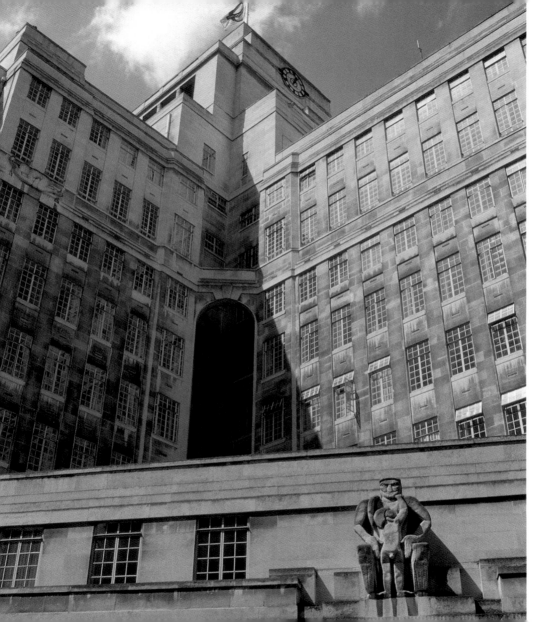

Broadway House,
London Passenger
Transport Board
Headquarters,
1927–29.
55 Broadway, SW1.
*A stepped-back cruciform
building in Portland stone.*
Architect:
Charles Holden.

Below:
*Cream glazed relief tile,
'55 Broadway'. 1938.*
Aldgate East
Underground Station,
Whitechapel High
Street, E1.
Sculptor:
Harold Stabler.

Broadway House.
Sculpture 'Day',
eastern entrance.
Sculptor:
Sir Jacob Epstein.

Jacob Epstein's first major
commission was for
Charles Holden's
British Medical Association
building in the Strand.
His sculptural figures were
later mutilated, but can still
be seen on what is now
Rhodesia House.

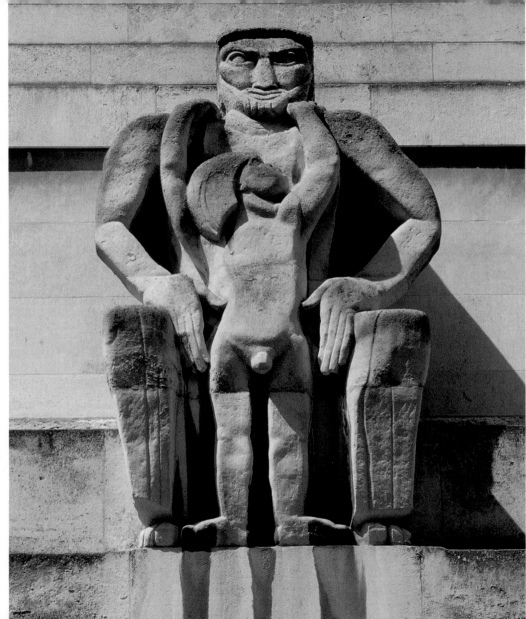

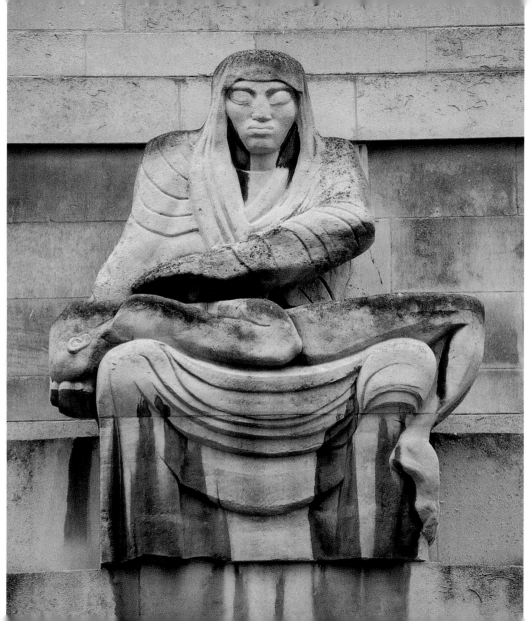

Broadway House.
Sculpture 'Night',
northern entrance.
Sculptor:
Sir Jacob Epstein.

The Daily Express
newspaper characterised
Epstein's 'Night' as
'a prehistoric blood-sodden
cannibal intoning a horrid
ritual over a dead victim'.

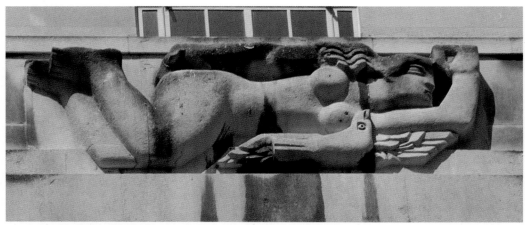

Top:
Broadway House.
'West Wind', on the
south side of the East Wing.
Sculptor:
Samuel Rabinovitch.

Other works by
Samuel Rabinovitch
include the façade of
the Daily Telegraph
building, Fleet Street
(page 34).

Below:
Broadway House.
'South Wind', on the
east side of the North Wing.
Sculptor: Eric Gill.

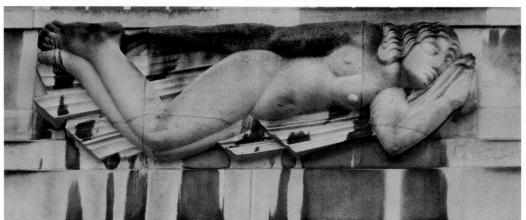

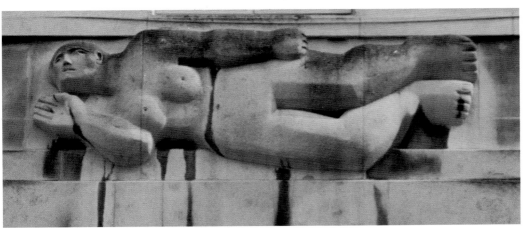

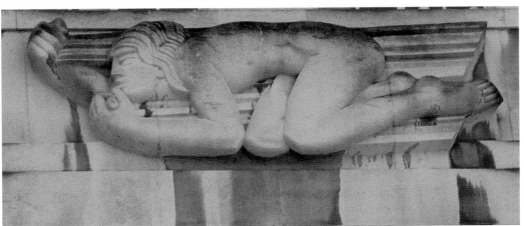

Top:
Broadway House.
*'West Wind', on the north
side of the East Wing.*
Sculptor: Henry Moore.

*Henry Moore, who favoured
sculpture in the round,
said that he only accepted
two to three commissions
in his entire career.*

Below:
Broadway House.
*'North Wind', on the east
side of the South Wing.*
Sculptor: Eric Gill.

*The relief sculptures, all
cut on site, also include
those created by
Eric Aumonier, A.H. Gerrard
and Allan Wyon.*

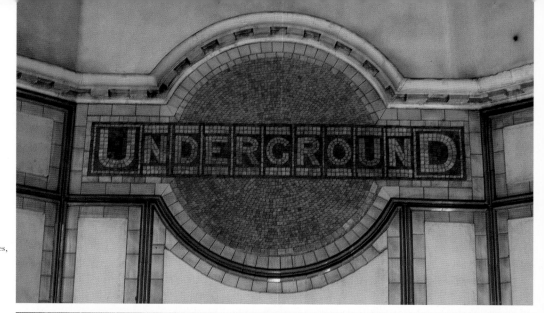

Top:
Maida Vale
Underground Station,
1915.
Bakerloo Line,
Edgware, W9.
Art Nouveau-style mosaic
'Bullseye', a precurser
to Edward Johnston's
Underground symbol of
1916–19.

Below:
Embankment
Underground Station,
District and Circle Lines,
WC2.
The 'Underground
Bullseye', 1919,
designed by
Edward Johnston,
incorporates his
London Transport
sans serif typeface
'Johnston Sans', 1916.

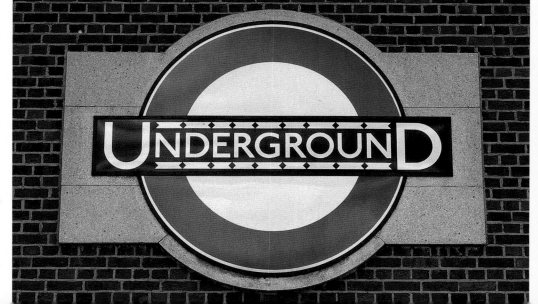

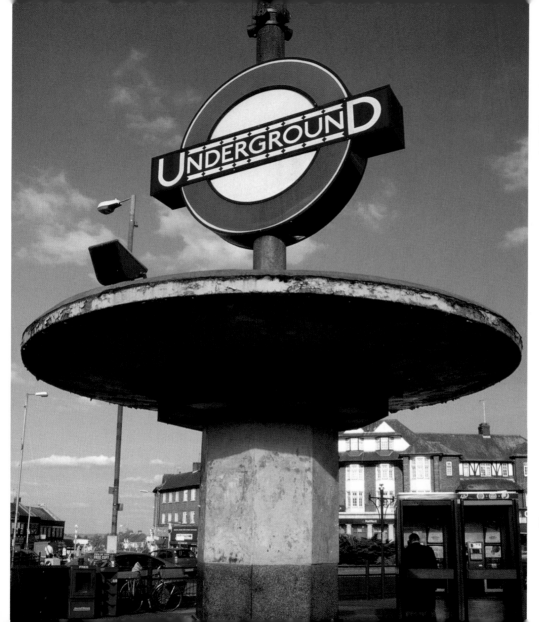

Southgate
Underground Station,
1933.
Piccadilly Line,
Southgate, N.14.
Architect:
Charles Holden.

101

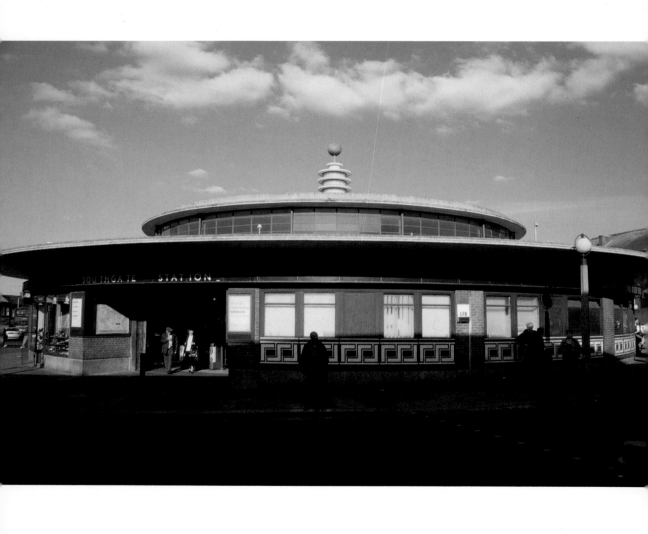

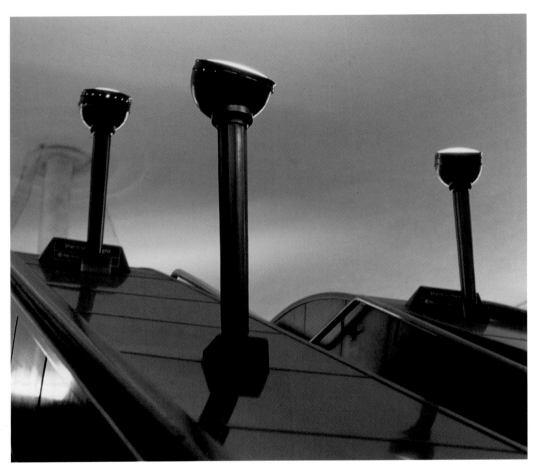

This page:
Southgate
Underground Station.
*Bronze uplighters centred
between the escalators.*

Opposite:
Southgate
Underground Station
and Shopping Centre,
1933.
Southgate, N14.
*Curved arcade of
shops and bus station.*
Architect:
Charles Holden of Adams,
Holden and Pearson.

This page:

Morden
Underground Station.
Northern Line.
*Brass chandelier in
the ticket hall.*

Opposite:
Metal ventilation grilles:

Top:
Manor House
Underground Station,
1932.
Piccadilly Line.
Green Lanes, N4.

Bottom:
Wood Green
Underground Station,
1932.
Piccadilly Line.
High Road, N22.

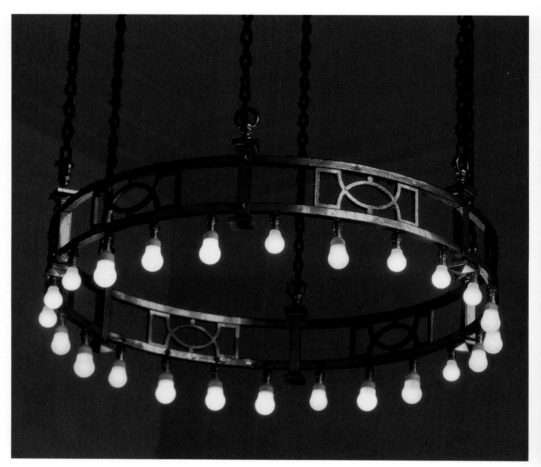

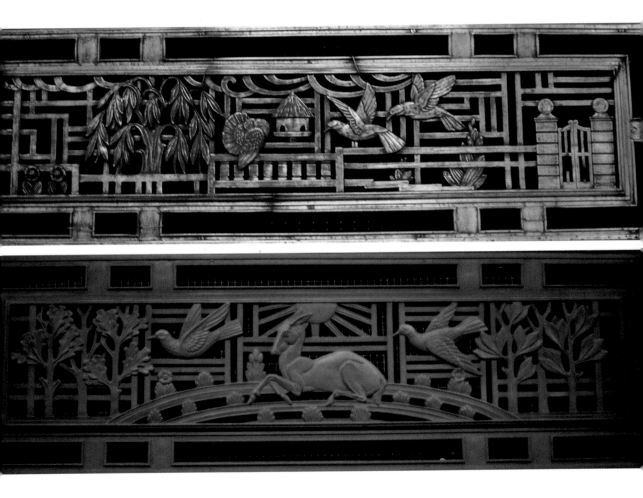

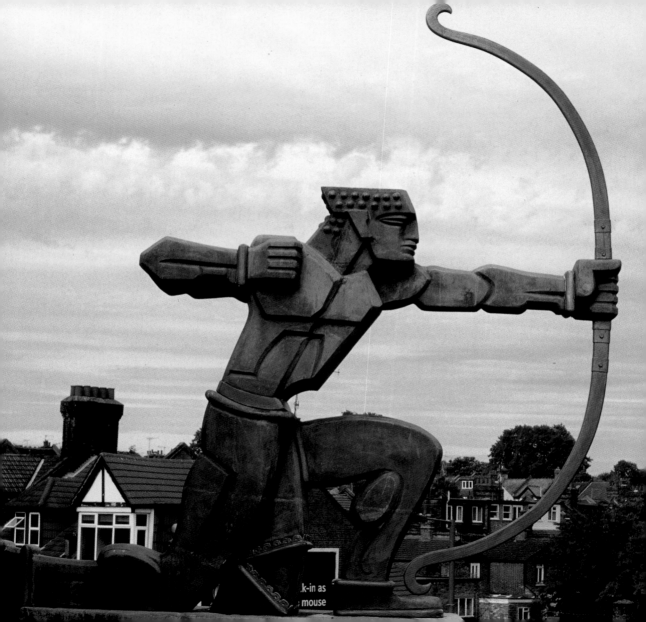

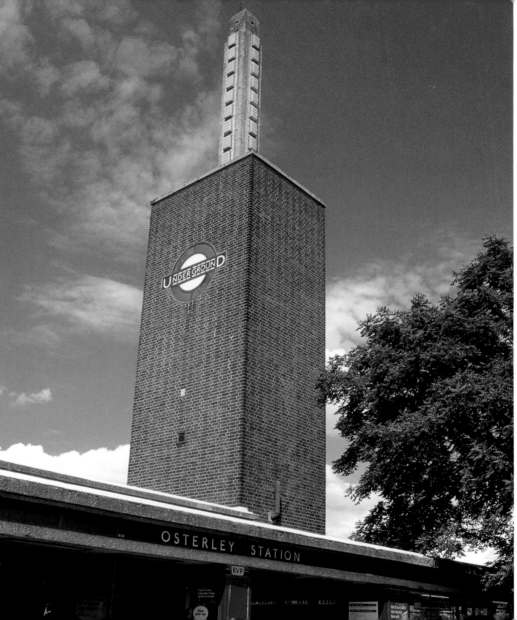

OSTERLEY STATION

RVP

This page:
Osterley
Underground Station,
1934,
Piccadilly Line,
Great West Road, TW7.
70-foot tower.
Architects:
Charles Holden
with S.A. Heaps.

Opposite:
East Finchley
Underground Station,
1940.
Northern Line.
Great North Road, N2.
'Archie', a three-dimensional
sculpture portrays an ancient
hunter, and is located
alongside one of the
railway tracks of East Finchley
Underground Station.
(Finchley was on the edge of
the royal forest of Enfield.)
The sculpture, made of 6cwt
beech round steel support,
is covered with 5cwt of
sheet lead. The bow was
made of English ash, bent
by steam and coated with
copper and gilt.
Sculptor: Eric Aumonier.

107

Right:
Sudbury Town
Underground Station,
1930–33.
Piccadilly Line,
Sudbury Town,
Greenford, Middlesex.
*A red brick and glass
ticket hall.*
Architect:
Charles Holden.

Below:
Sudbury Town
Underground Station.
Weather gauge.

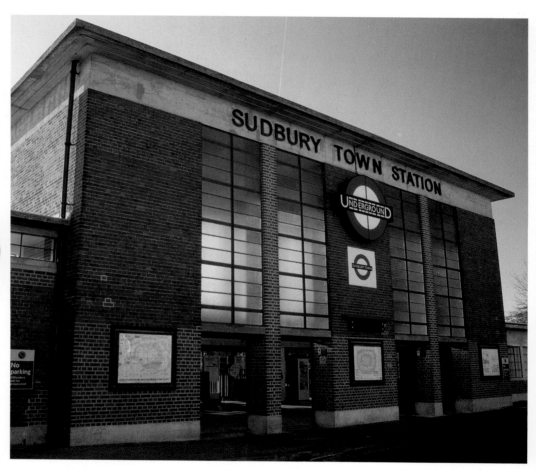

108

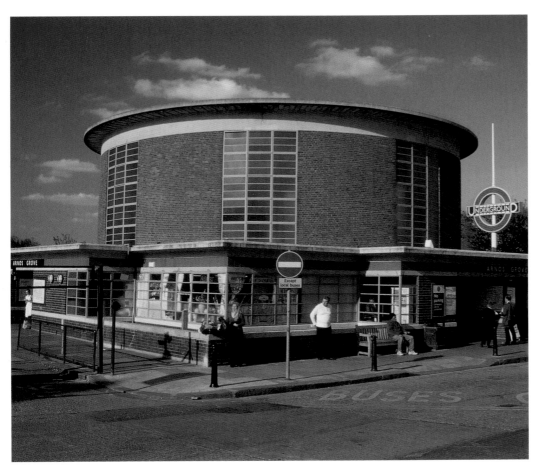

Arnos Grove
Underground station,
1932–33.
Piccadilly Line,
Bowes Road, N11.
Drum-shaped ticket hall,
said to be inspired by
the Stockholm City Library,
1928.
Architect:
Charles Holden.

Institutional & Civic Buildings

Walthamstow
Town Hall, 1938–41.
Forest Road, E17.
*Portland stone and
copper clock tower.
Columns flanking the
building's entrance
are decorated with
bas-reliefs.*

*Other town halls
decorated with
bas-reliefs include
Bethnal Green, Poplar
and Wandsworth.*

'LONDON IS INDEED A THOUSAND VILLAGES; remove them and all that is left is a vast hulk peppered with spectacular buildings…' – Ian Nairn.

After the Second World War, London's civic authorities set about to build a string of impressive town halls: Hornsey to the north, Hammersmith to the west, Greenwich to the east and Wandsworth to the south, among others. Mosaics and sculptural reliefs often spelled out the history of their boroughs.

Other civic institutions built at that time include health centres, schools, libraries, and fire and police stations, employing the best architects, designers and sculptors of the day.

The former Royal Masonic Hospital's red brick and glass construction very much echoes continental buildings of the period. The hospital's main doors are decorated with acid-etched glass with the signs of the zodiac and flanked by two pylons surmounted by concrete figures of 'Healing' and 'Charity'.

One of the finest tributes to the artisans of the day is G. Grey Wornum's Royal Institute of British Architects in Portland Place. London University's Senate House was designed by Charles Holden, who was instructed that under no circumstances was he to employ Jacob Epstein, due to the public outcry of the sculptor's previous work. Holden, on being offered a knighthood, declined, stating that it would separate him from the ordinary people.

110

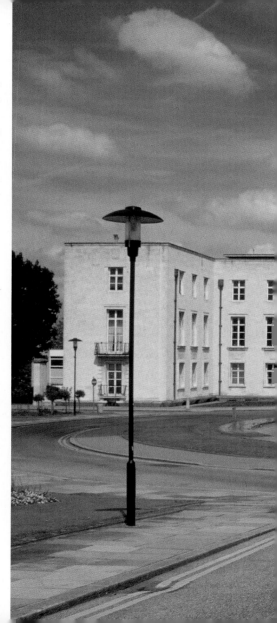

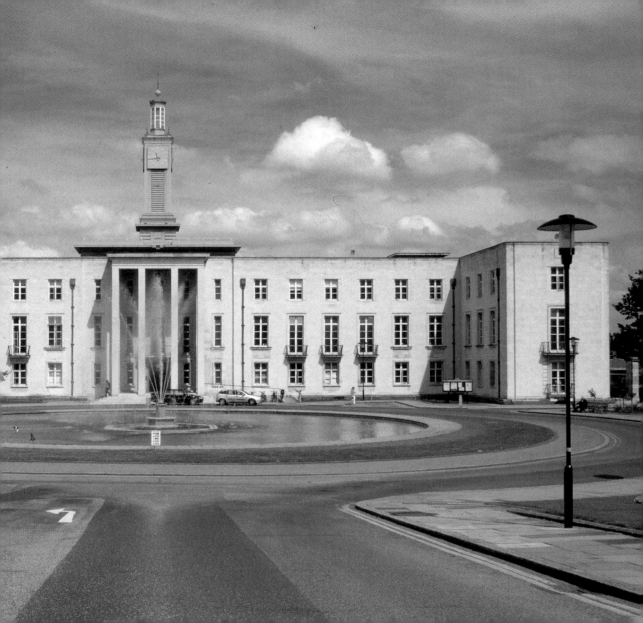

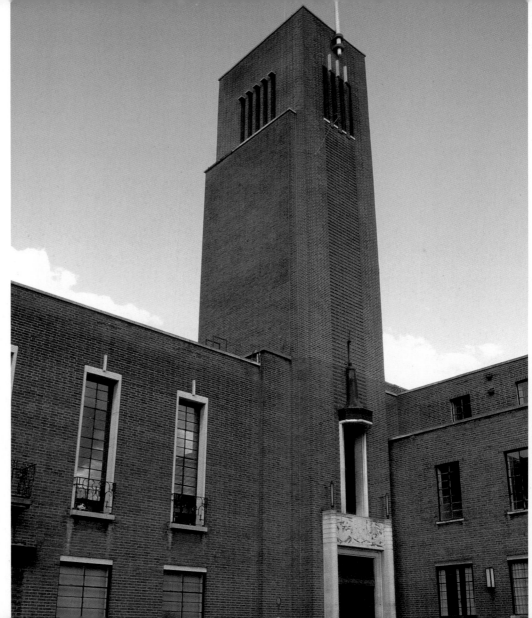

This page:
Hornsey Town Hall,
1934–35.
The Broadway,
Crouch End, N8.
The Hornsey Town Hall's
brick tower was inspired by
Willem Marinus Dudok's
design of Hilversum
Town Hall (1924–30),
the Netherlands.
Architects:
R.M. Uren, Slate
& Moberley.

Opposite:
Hornsey Town Hall.
Decorative cast metal
entrance gates.
Sculptor: A. J. Ayres.

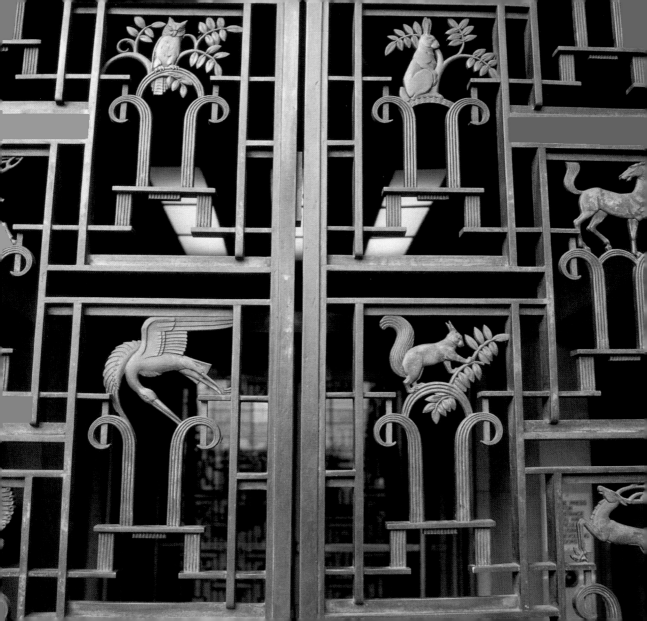

Hornsey Town Hall.
*Four of a number of
Portland stone bas-relief
panels on the walls of
the Gas and Electricity
showrooms added to the
Town Hall in 1935–37.*
Sculptor: A. J. Ayres.

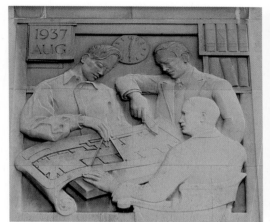
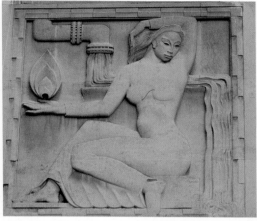
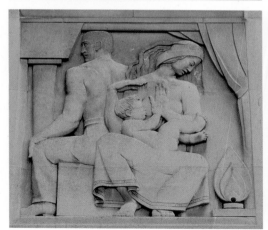
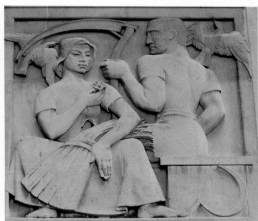

114

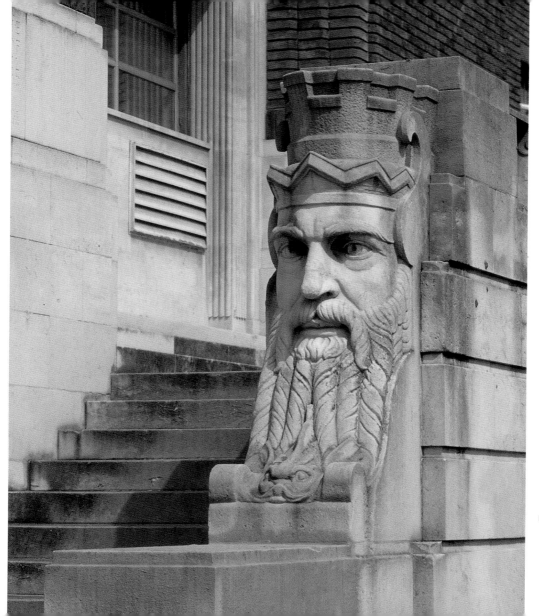

Hammersmith
Town Hall, 1939.
King Street, W6.
"Father Thames",
Portland stone balustrade.
Architect:
E. Berry Webber.
Sculptor:
George Alexander.

This page and opposite:
Greenwich Town Hall,
1939.
(Now Greenwich
Dance Agency)
Royal Hill, SE10.
*Mosaic ceiling to
entrance-way features a
telescope and ship, paying
homage to Greenwich's
Observatory and seafaring
heritage. This design is
surrounded by the signs
of the Zodiac.
These mosaic zodiacs are
reminiscent of those on
the 6th century Beit Alpha
synagogue floor, Israel.*
Architects:
Ewart Culpin & Son.

*Stained glass windows
decorated with the signs
of the zodiac also adorn
Sir Owen Williams'
'zig-zag' designed
Dollis Hill Synagogue
(1937),
now a primary school,
Park Side, Dollis Hill,
NW2.*

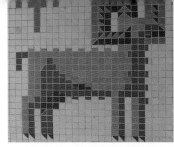
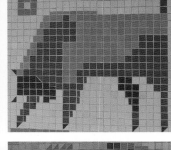
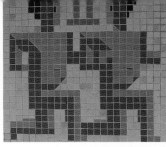
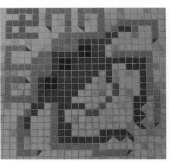
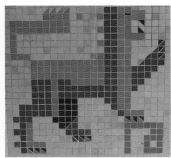
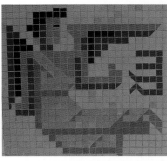
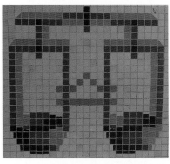
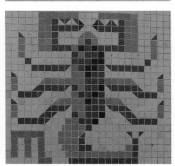
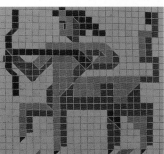
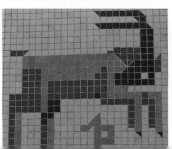
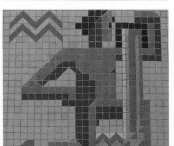
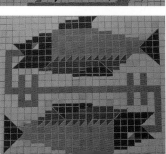

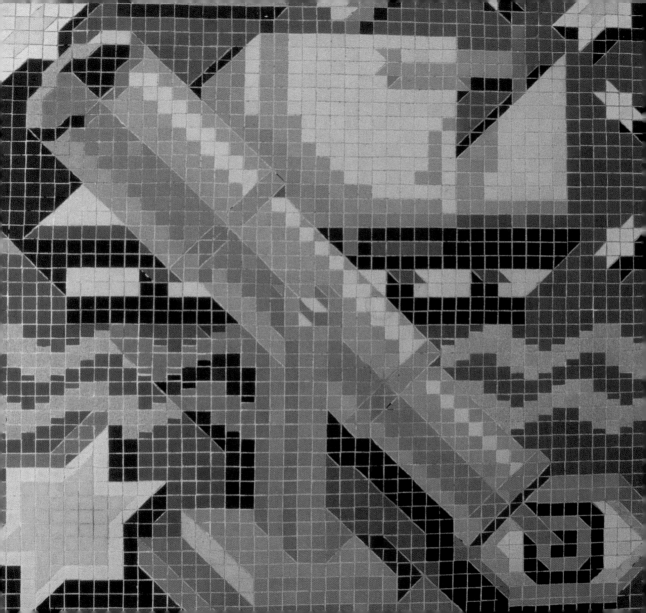

This page and opposite:
Royal Masonic Hospital,
1931–33.
(Now Stamford Hospital)
Ravenscourt Park, W6.
Acid etched glass windows
with zodiac signs.
Sculptor:
Gilbert William Bayes, RA.
Architects:
Sir John Burnet,
Tait and Lorne.

Lubetkin and Tecton's
Finsbury Health Centre
(1938–39) was depicted
in Abram Games' poster
'Your Britain Fight for
it Now'. The poster was
banned by Prime Minister
Winston Churchill for
depicting a slum labelled
'Disease' and 'Neglect'
behind the health centre's
façade. Ironically, for a
period this building fell into
neglect, almost resembling
the slum in the poster.

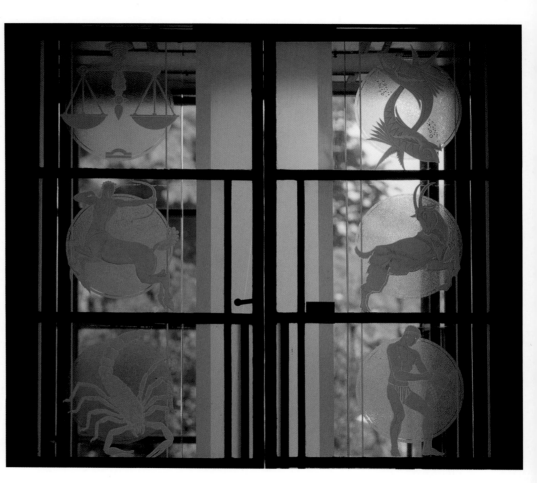

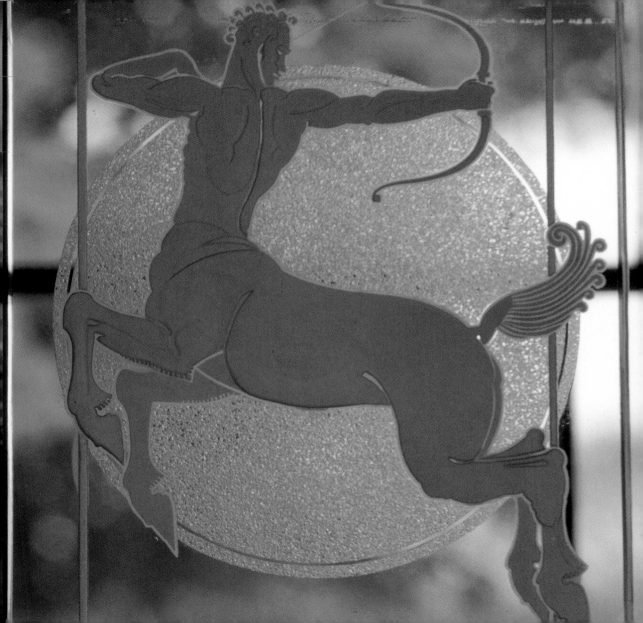

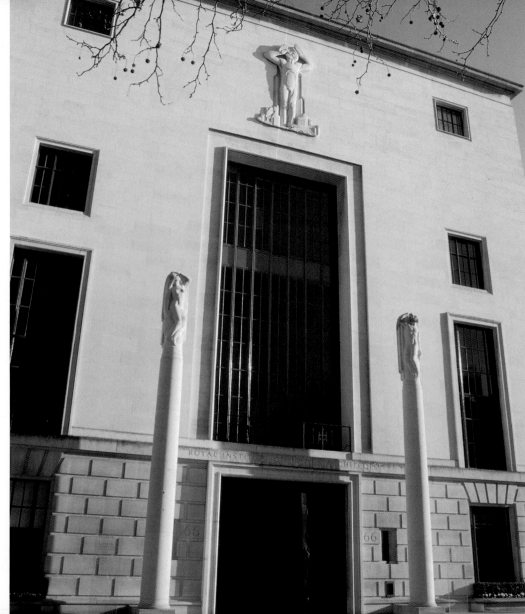

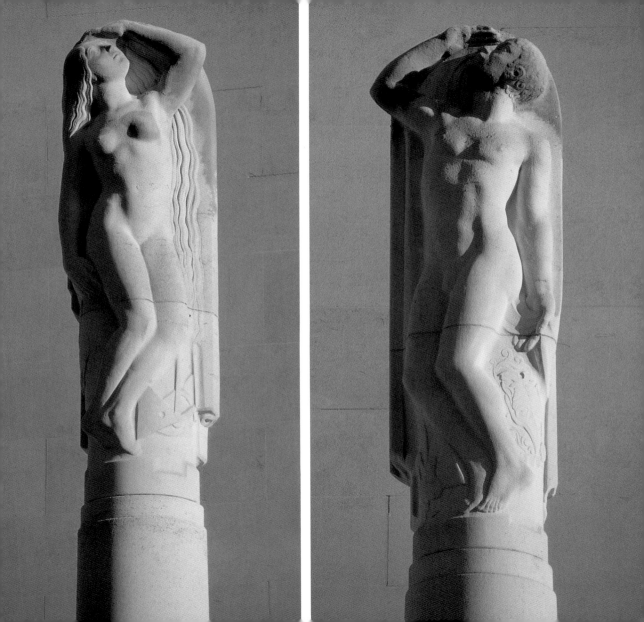

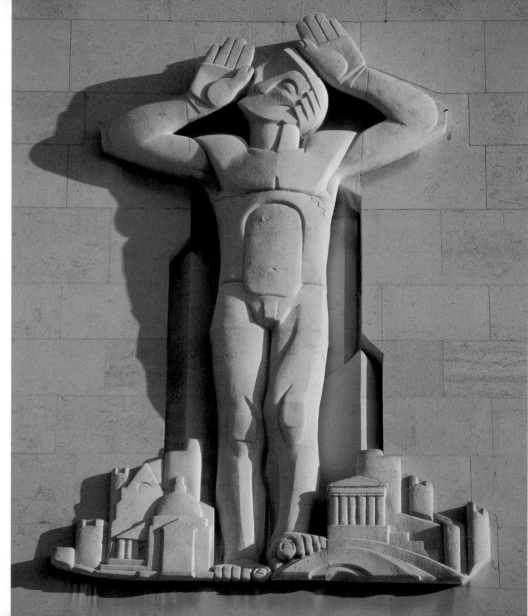

This page:
Royal Institute of
British Architects.
*Portland stone figure
'Architectural aspiration'.*
Sculptor:
Bainbridge Copnall.

Opposite:
Royal Institute of
British Architects.
*'London's Rivers and its
Buildings', 12-feet-high,
one and a half-ton
cast bronze doors, which
include the images of the
Houses of Parliament,
St. James's Palace,
the Guildhall,
St. Paul's Cathedral,
Regent's Park Zoo,
Waterloo Bridge,
the Serpentine,
a London Underground
tunnel and a
London County Council
tenement building.*
Sculptor:
James Woodford, RA.

122

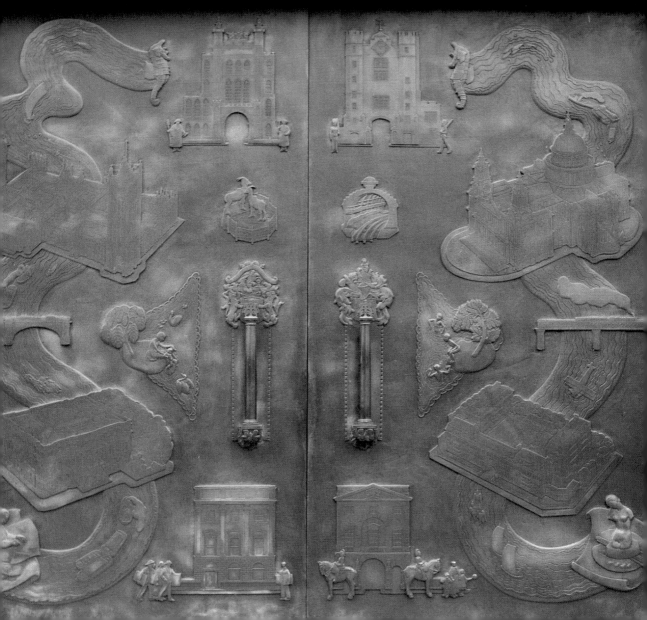

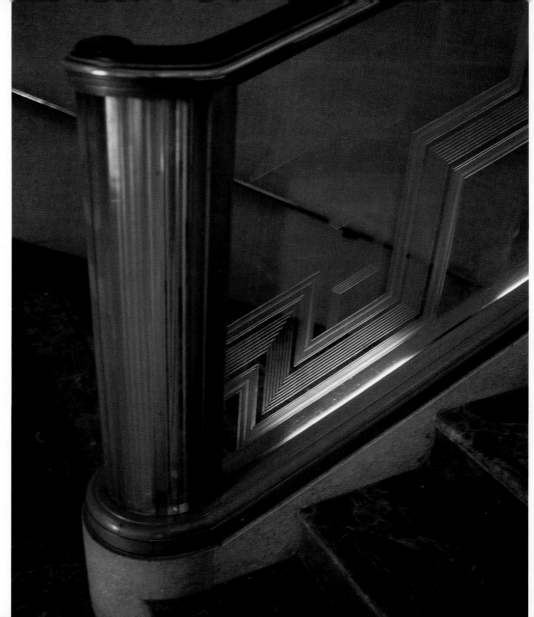

This page:
Royal Institute of
British Architects.
Etched glass balustrade.

Opposite:
Royal Institute of
British Architects.
*Etched glass doors leading
into Florence Hall,
engraved by Jan Juta.*

124

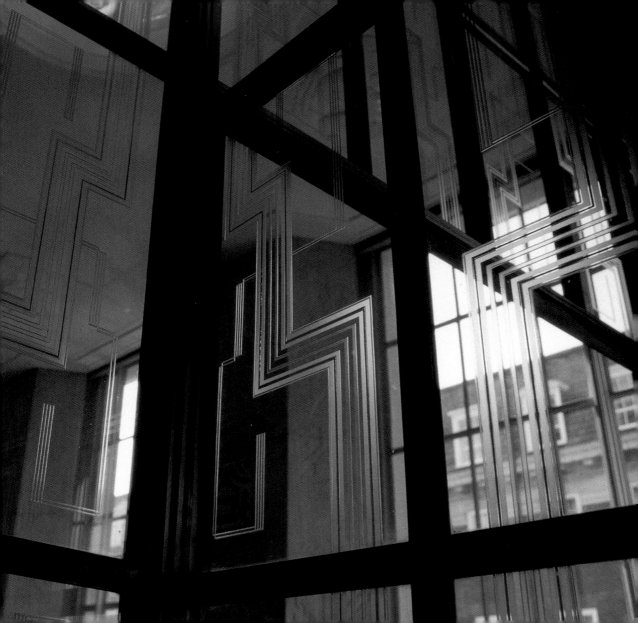

This page:
Senate House,
University of London,
1932.
Malet Street and
Montague Place, WC1.
Metal and glass lamp
on the main gate posts
to Senate House.
Architect:
Charles Holden.

Opposite:
Senate House.
The 12-floor, 210-foot-high
stepped Portland stone
building is London's first
skyscraper. Its first floor is
clad with Cornish granite.
The building and its
neighbouring School of
Hygiene and Tropical
Medicine (page 128) were
badly damaged during
air-raids in 1940.

126

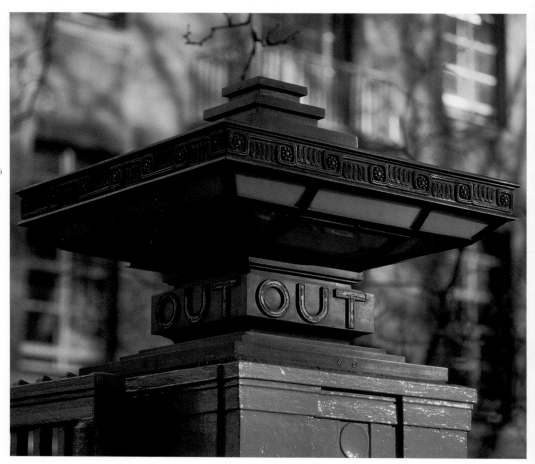

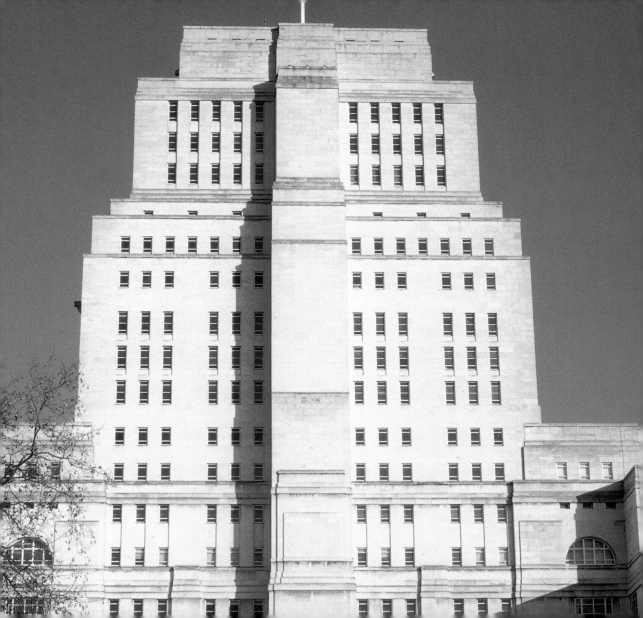

School of Hygiene and
Tropical Medicine,
University of London,
1926–28.
Gower Street and
Keppel Street, WC1,
*Decorative gilded metal
insects on the balconies.*
Architects:
Morely Horder and
Vernon Rees.

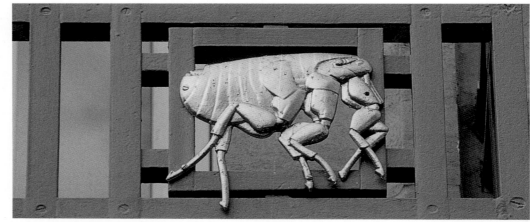

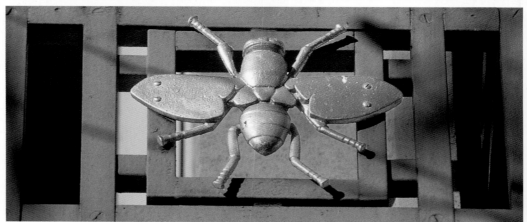

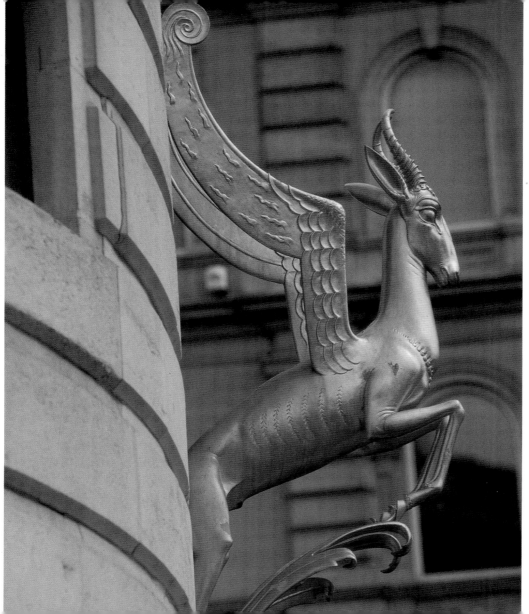

South Africa House,
1930–35.
Trafalgar Square and
Strand, WC2.
Gilded leaping springbok.
The six-storey building
was erected on the former
site of Morey's Hotel.
Sculptor: Sir Charles
Thomas Wheeler, RA.
Architect:
Sir Herbert Baker.

129

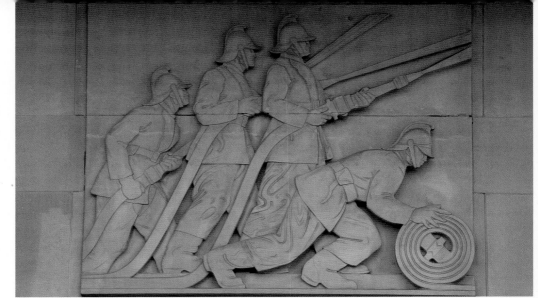

This page:
London Fire Brigade
Headquarters, 1937.
8 Albert Embankment,
SE1.
Two Portland stone panels
above the north
and south entrances.
Sculptor:
S. Nicholson Babb.

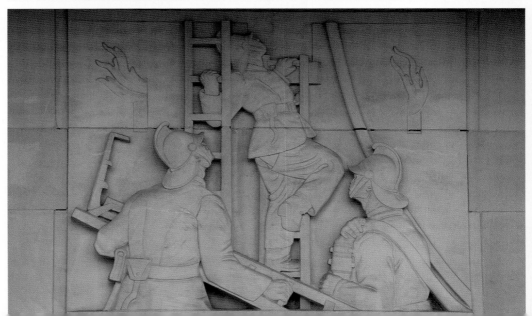

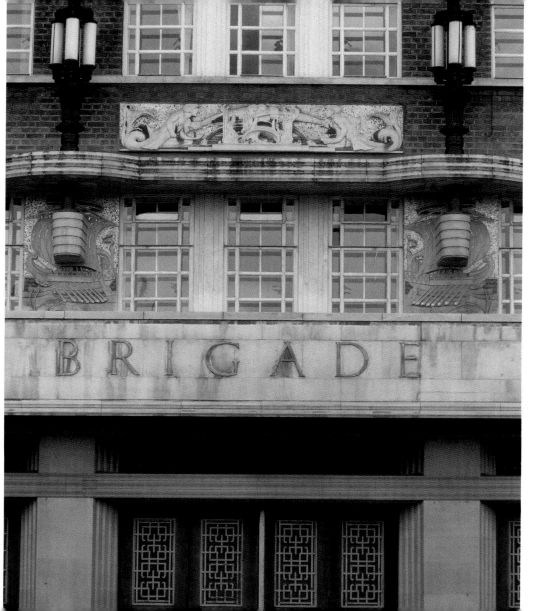

London Fire Brigade
Headquarters.
*Façade with gilded
reliefs and lanterns.*
Sculptor: Gilbert Bayes.

*London Fire Brigade
Headquarters' neighbouring
nine-storey W.H. Smith
booksellers headquarters
(1936) with its
150-foot illuminated
clock tower has since
been demolished.*

131

Residential Buildings

50 Sloane Street, SW1.
1930s.
*Multi-storey flats
and shop promenade.
Other notable residential
buildings include
Guy Morgan & Partners'
Florin Court, (1936),
Charterhouse Street, EC1.
Florin Court appeared as
Whitehaven Mansions, the
fictional home of Agatha
Christie's Hercules Poirot, in
the 1980s television series.
Design patron Jack Pritchard
commissioned Wells Coates
to design the Isokon
(Isometric Unit Construction)
cooperative flats, (1933–34)
Lawn Road, Hampstead.
Architectural historian
Nikolaus Pevsner
referred to the project as
'giant's work of the 1930s'.
Among the Isokon residents
were Walter Gropius,
Marcel Breuer
and Agatha Christie.
No. 2 Willow Road,
Erno Goldfinger's former
home at his terraced
housing project, is
open to the public.*

'THE STATELY HOMES OF ENGLAND, how beautiful they stand!' – Felicia Hemans.

English Heritage are now the guardians of the medieval Eltham Palace. Its interior was transformed into an elegant Art Deco home by Seeley and Paget in the 1930s.

The semi-detached, sunrise, suntrap curved metal bay-windowed homes of suburbia are humorously depicted in James Fitton's map of 1929 with the legend: 'Sorry, it's deadly dull here – houses and houses and houses.'

With the extension of the Underground system in the inter-war years, Greater London's population rose by over one million inhabitants. The need for new housing brought about a boom in construction, from the working-class Council-subsidized dwellings, such as Sir Edwin Lutyen's Grosvenor Estate (1928–30), Westminster, to luxury flats and individual residences. Among the most innovative housing projects were Wells Coates's Isokon flats (1933–34); Maxwell Fry's Sun House (1936); and Erno Goldfinger's 1–3 Willow Road (1939) in Hampstead. Others were Lubetkin and Tecton's residential blocks High Point One and Two (1933–38), Highgate; Stanley Gordon Jeeves' huge Dolphin Square (1937), Grosvenor Road; and Guy Morgan & Partners' Florin Court (1936), Farringdon, which Nikolaus Pevsner aptly described as 'poised between Modernism and Art Deco'.

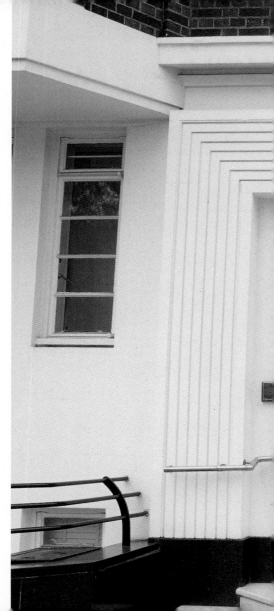

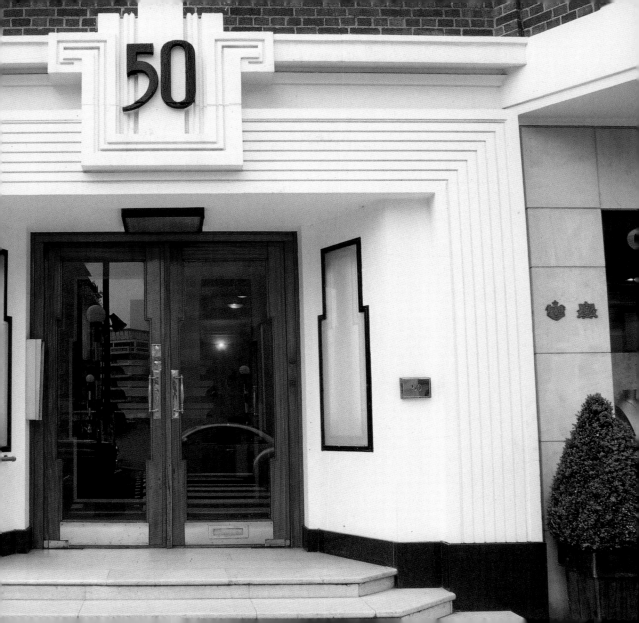

This page:
Dorset House, 1935.
Baker Street and
Melcombe Street, NW1.
*A ten-storey red brick,
plaster and steel
residential building.*
Architects:
Bennett, T.P. &
Joseph Emberton.

Opposite:
Dorset House.
*Two bas reliefs flank
the front entrance.*
Sculptor: Eric Gill.

*Joseph Emberton
also designed the
Stuart Mills House
(1937).
Killick Street, N1.*

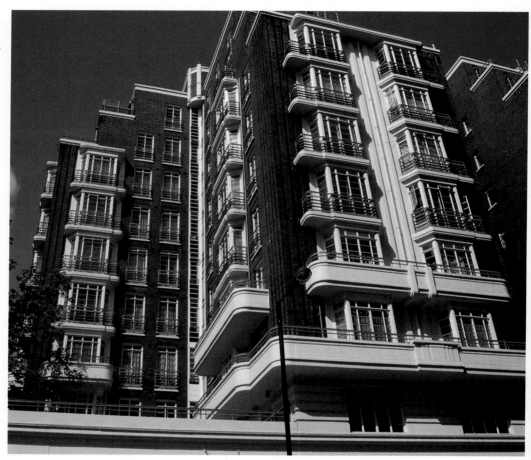

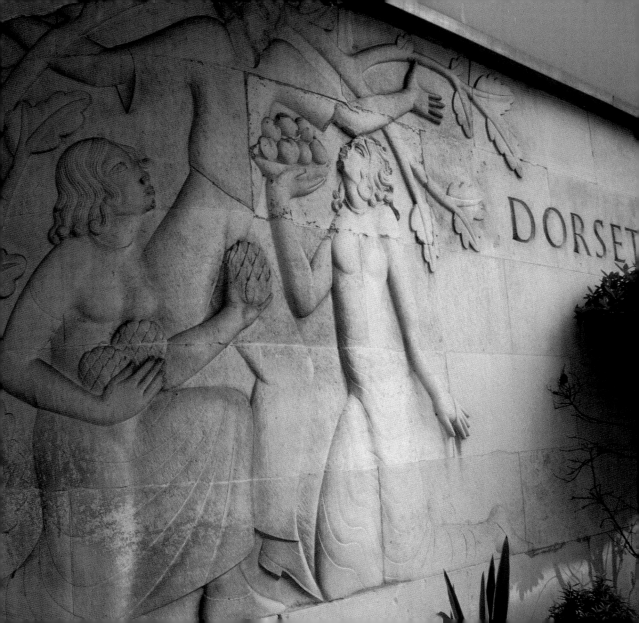

Memorials

Hudson Memorial,
1923.
North side of
Hyde Park, W2.
Author W. H. Hudson's
most famous character,
'Rima', on the much
maligned memorial.
Sculptor:
Sir Jacob Epstein.
Inscription by Eric Gill.

'HERE WAS A ROYAL FELLOWSHIP OF DEATH.' This chilling epitaph is inscribed upon the Royal Artillery War memorial at Hyde Park. Its creators, Charles Sargeant Jagger and Lionel Pearson, are some of the greatest sculptors that graced the face of London of that time. Other luminaries include Eric Gill and Sir Jacob Epstein, whose sculptures were ubiquitous. Epstein's works were constantly dogged by criticism and anti-semitism, however he was later described as the twentieth century's greatest sculptor.

Epstein had worked with architect Charles Holden on the British Medical Association's building in the Strand. When it was later taken over as Rhodesia House, his sculptural pieces were mutilated. Among his most controversial work was his interpretation of 'Rima' on the Hudson Memorial in Hyde Park, it was twice smeared with tar and feathers, and escaped a lobbed bomb. A gang of hooligans also threw a jar of tar at his sculpture of 'Night' at Broadway House, but missed its target.

Other significant memorials are those of Sir Edwin Lutyen's Cenotaph in Whitehall, commemorating those who died in the First World War.

Sir George Frampton's memorial to Edith Cavell (1920–24) in St. Martin's Place is inscribed with: 'Patriotism is not enough', and in Holborn stands Alfred Toft's bronze memorial to the Royal Fusiliers, City of London Regiment (1922).

136

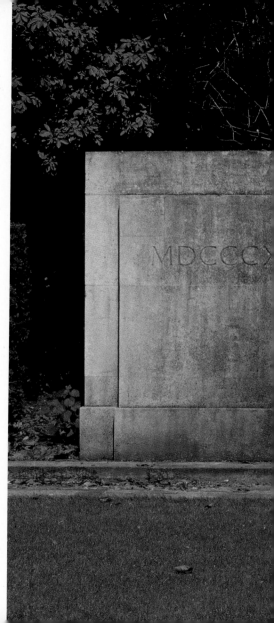

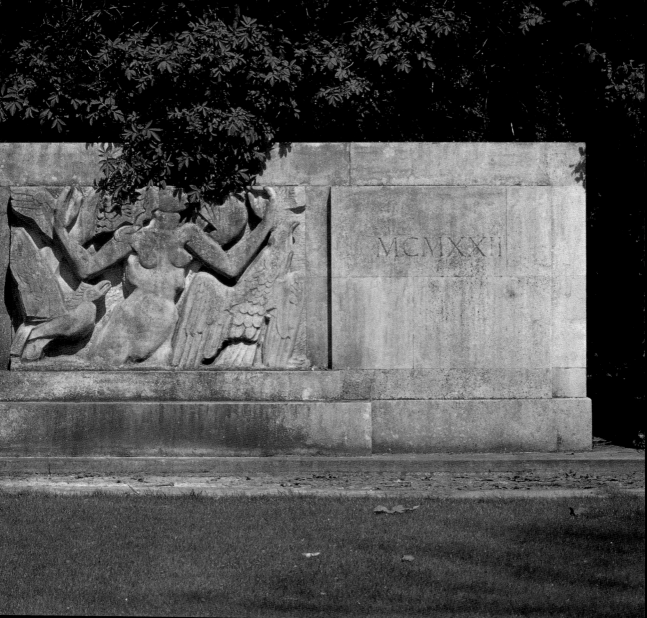

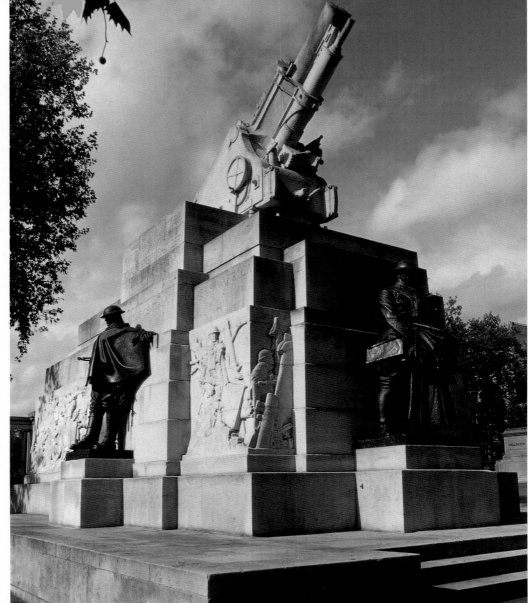

Royal Artillery
Memorial, 1925.
Hyde Park Corner, W1.
Built of Portland stone,
and flanked on four sides
by bronze artillerymen
beneath a life-size
9.2 inch Howitzer
gun, facing the
Somme battlefield, France.
Sculptors:
Charles Sargeant Jagger
and Lionel Pearson.

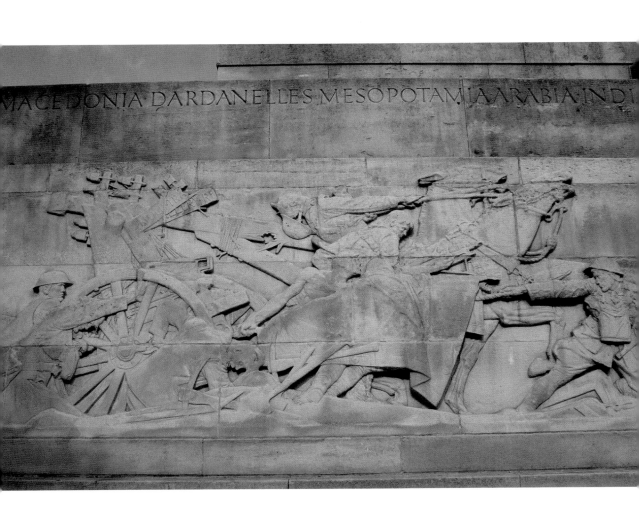

MACEDONIA DARDANELLES MESOPOTAMIA ARABIA INDI

Factories

The London Power Company's Battersea Power Station, 1934. Kirtling Street, SW8. *Red brick with stone fluted chimney stacks.* Architects: Halliday and Agate, with Sir Giles Gilbert Scott. Engineer: S.L. Pearce.

In 2013, a Malaysian consortium purchased the iconic power station with plans to redevelop the site into homes, offices and shops.

'CONCRETE, METAL, GLASS, AND PLYWOOD are the "big four" of modern architecture.' – Sir Gilbert Scott.

Sir Gilbert, the architect of the futuristic icons of Battersea and Bankside power stations, which were dubbed 'cathedrals of the twentieth century', also designed Liverpool Cathedral, the Guinness Brewery and the rapidly disappearing red telephone kiosk.

A second industrial revolution had begun in the aftermath of the First World War and the power stations were the source of energy for the numerous new factories serving the hub of the Empire.

A good number of these factories were built on what became known as the 'Golden Mile' along the Great West Road, the location giving convenient road and rail access to Southampton and the docks. Architects Wallis, Gilbert and Partners designed the Hoover, Coty, and Pyrene factories, and the jewel in the crown was their Firestone Tyre and Rubber Company building. Others of note were Sir Banister Fletcher's Gillette factory, and the Macleans, Wrigley, Chrysler and Packard factories.

Of the Hoover factory art historian Bevis Hillier, in his book *World of Art Deco,* (1971), posed the question 'Ballet Russe, Aztec or Egyptian?'. Unlike the Firestone factory, the Hoover building thankfully survives. In central London, two outstanding examples remain, the Carreras Black Cat Cigarette factory and the Oxo building, albeit in new incarnations.

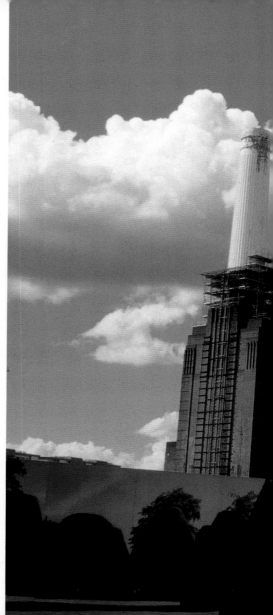

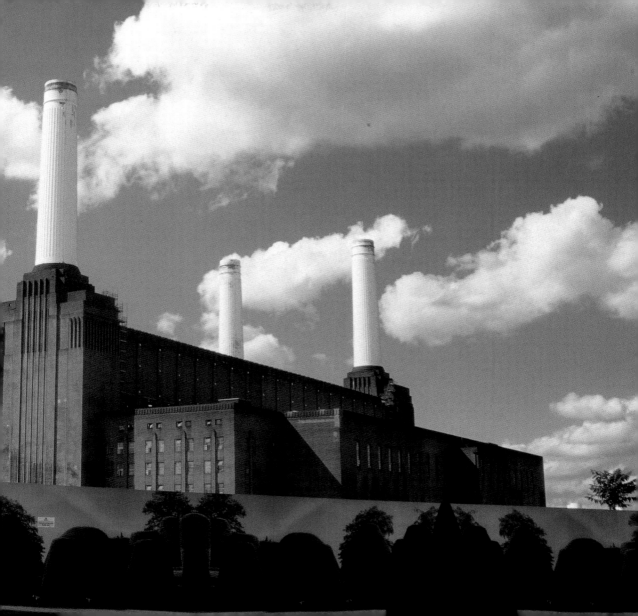

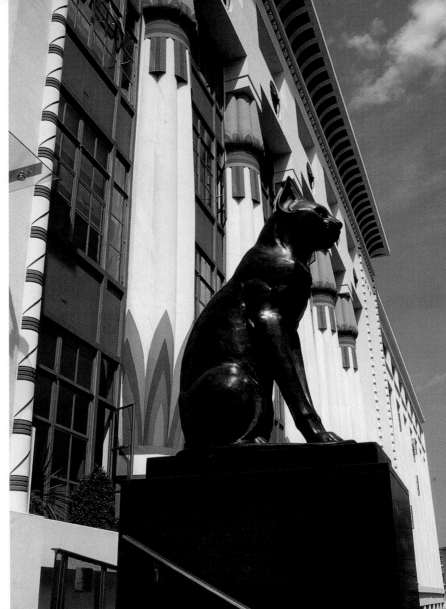

This page and opposite:
Carreras
Cigarette Factory, 1928.
Hampstead Road, NW1.
*Two 8-foot high black cats
stand as sentinels at
the main entrance.
The 'Black Cat'
cigarette factory's design
was inspired by
the discovery of
Tutankhamen's Tomb
by Lord Carnarvon and
Howard Carter in 1922.
The façade was stripped
of its decorations in the
1960s to become Greater
London House, and
restored to its original
state in 1999.*
Architects:
M.E. & O.H. Collins
with A.G. Porri.

142

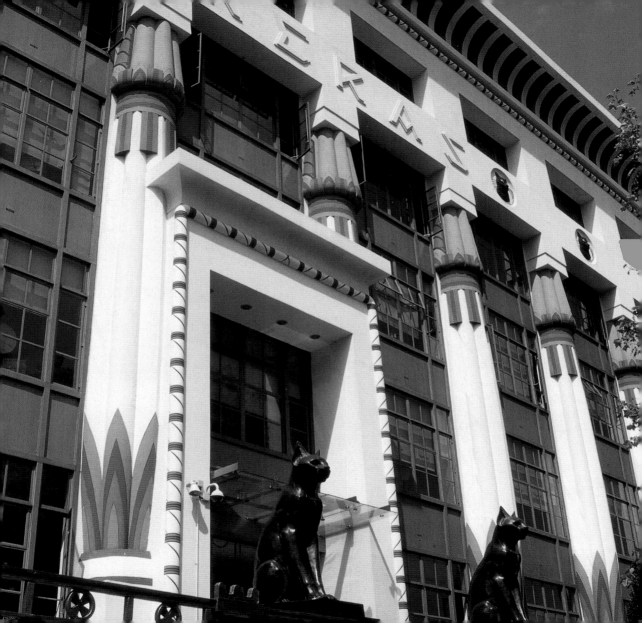

This page:
Oxo Tower, 1928.
Bargehouse Street, SE1.
(Restored in 1993,
now a restaurant
and shops).
Illuminated windows
circumvented restrictions
on illuminated signage
of the company name.
Architect:
Albert Walter Moore.

Opposite:
Firestone Tyre Factory,
1929.
Great West Road,
Osterley, TW7.
Apart from a few lamp
standards, these wrought
iron main gates are the
only remnants of this
magnificent property,
which was demolished on
the eve of becoming a
listed building in 1980.
Architects:
Wallis, Gilbert
and Partners.

144

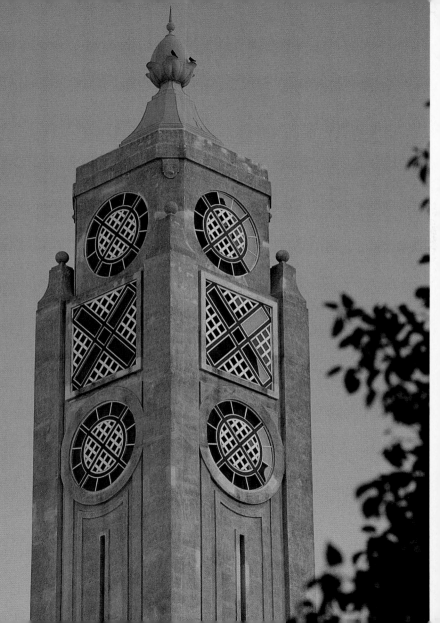

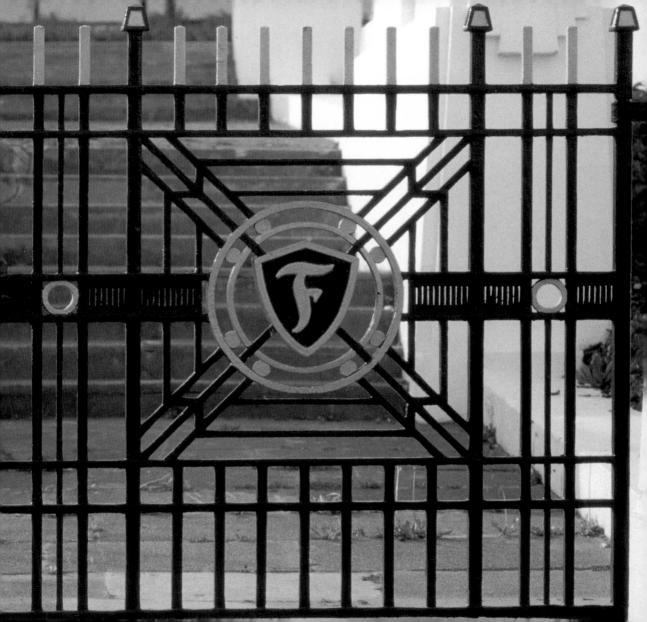

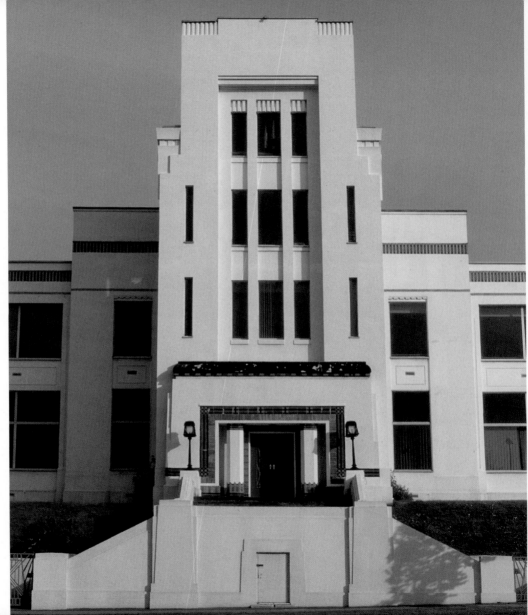

This page:
Pyrene Fire Extinguisher
Company Factory,
1929–30.
(Now BMW Building)
Great West Road,
Brentford, Middlesex.
*A reinforced concrete
zig-zag Moderne building.*
Architects:
Wallis, Gilbert
and Partners.

Opposite:
Coty Factory, c. 1932.
Great West Road,
Brentford, Middlesex,
Architects:
Wallis, Gilbert
and Partners.

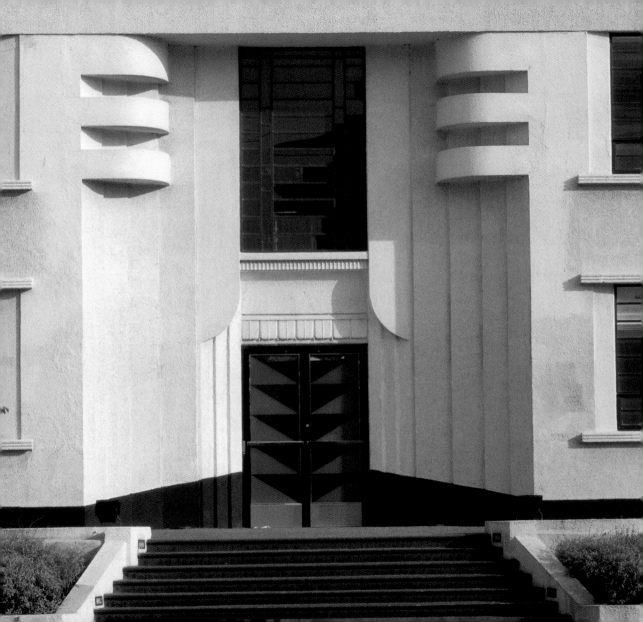

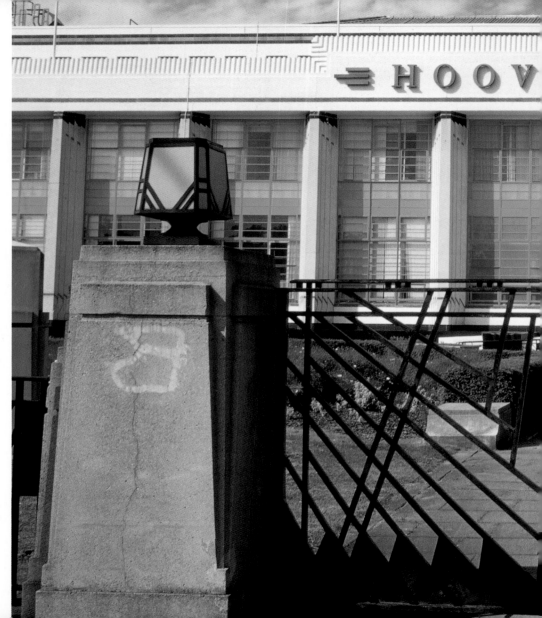

This page and opposite:
The Hoover Factory,
1931–35.
(Now a Tesco's
Superstore)
Western Avenue,
Perivale, Middlesex,
Accessible to the Great
Western Railway and
docks for distribution of
its vacuum cleaners,
the Hoover Factory
was constructed using
'Snowcreate' (a white
concrete which stays white
in spite of British weather)
and decorated with bright
coloured faïence ceramic
Egyptian-inspired tiles.
Architects:
Wallis, Gilbert
and Partners.

148

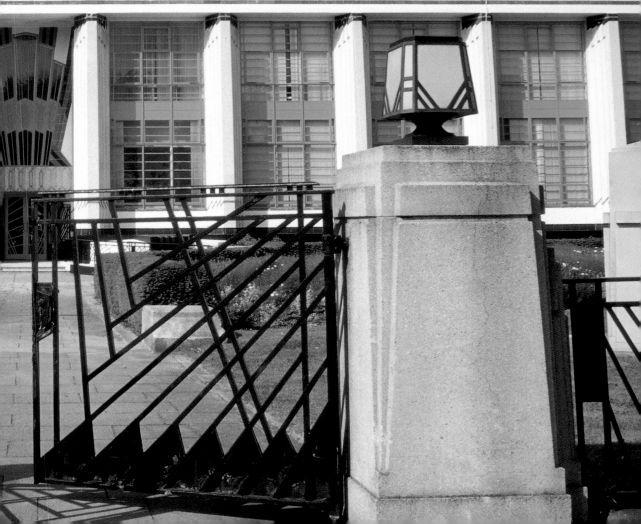

The Hoover Factory.
Main entrance.

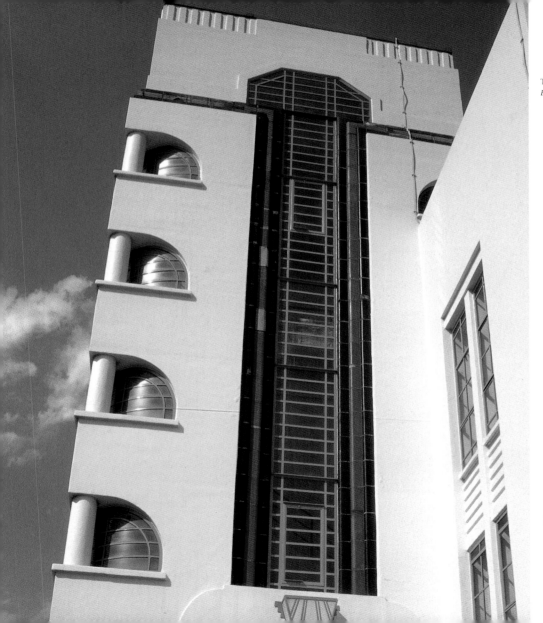

The Hoover Factory.
Exterior of the west wing.

151

The Hoover Factory.
Canteen building.

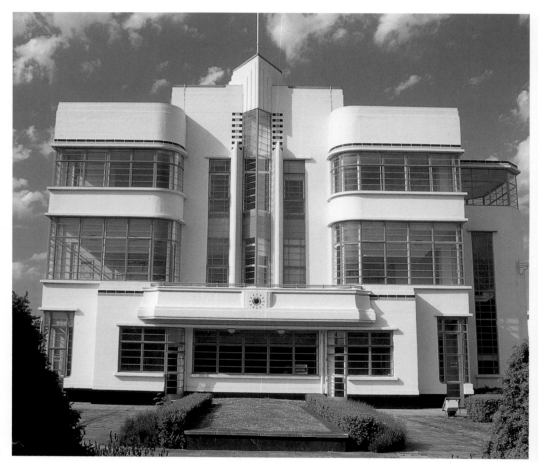

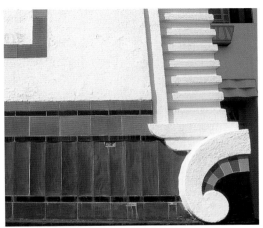
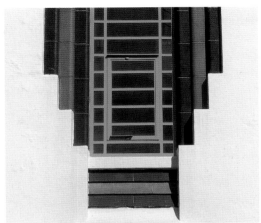

The Hoover Factory.
Architectural details.

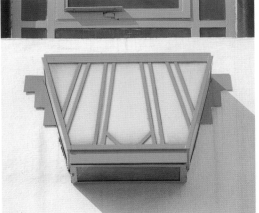
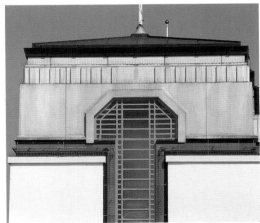

Lamps

Left:
Unilever House,
1930–32.
New Bridge Street, EC4.
Architect:
J. Lomax-Simpson
with Sir John Burnet,
Tait and Lorne.
Sculptor: Walter Gilbert

Centre above:
Daily Telegraph newspaper
building, 1928.
120 Fleet Street, EC4.

Centre:
The Hoover Factory,
1931–35.
Western Avenue,
Perivale, Middlesex.

Centre below:
Hackney Town Hall,
1934–36.
Mare Street,
Hackney, E8.

Right:
Firestone Tyre and
Rubber Company,
1929.
Great West Road,
Osterley, TW7.

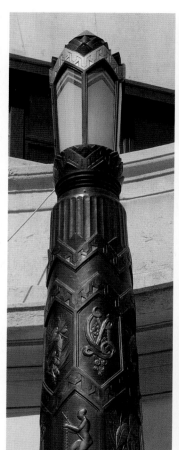

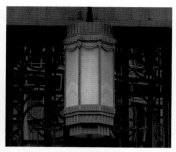

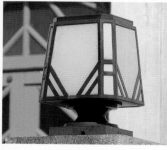

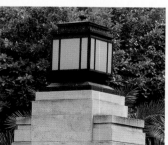

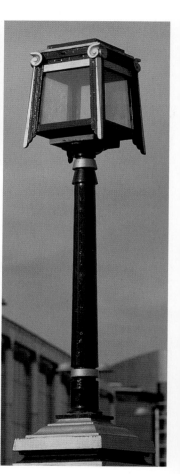

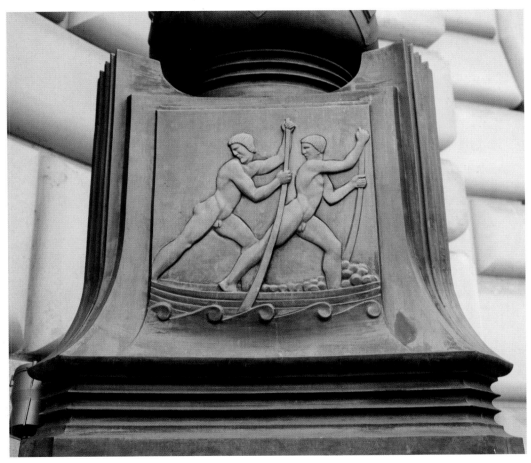

*Base of bronze
lamp standard.*
Unilever House, 1929.
100 Victoria
Embankment,
EC4.
*The work was modelled
by Walter Gilbert in
association with
Donald Gilbert in
1931 to 1932.*

155

Signage

This page:
Former Arsenal Football Grounds, 1932. Highbury Hill, N5. (Currently being redeveloped as luxury apartments) *West Gate metal signage.* Architects: Claude Ferrier and William Binnie.

Opposite:
Paddington Station, Great Western Railway, 1933. Eastbourne Terrace and Praed Street, W2. *Wrought iron window grille.* Architect: P.G. Culverhouse.

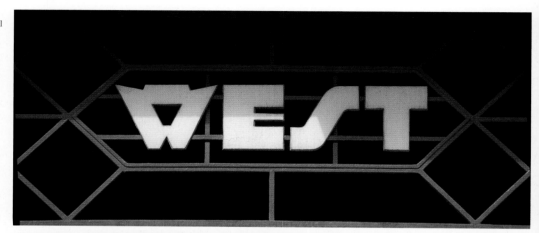

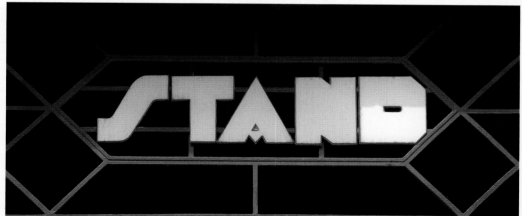

156

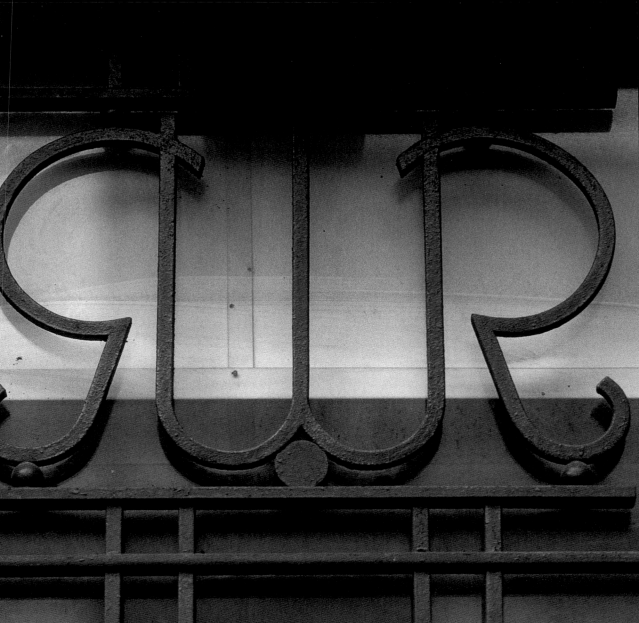

Modernising Britain

Opposite:
De La Warr Pavilion,
1935.
Bexhill on Sea,
East Sussex.
*Welded steel frame
and glass structure.
Exterior, seaside prospect.*
Architects:
Eric Mendelsohn
and Serge Chermayeff.

Overleaf:
De La Warr Pavilion.
*South staircase with
central light fitting.*

*By the late 1920s,
Erich Mendelsohn was
considered Germany's
leading architect, a
designer of factories and
several large department
stores for the
Schocken Company.
Russian-born interior
designer Serge Chermayeff
was educated at Harrow
School and first achieved
prominence as the director of
the Modern Art Department
of Waring and Gillow's
furniture store.*

'A NEW STYLE WILL ASSERT ITSELF'. – Le Corbusier. The 'International Style', as it became known, focused on the 'machine aesthetic' and is a distillation of the German *Bauhaus* and Dutch *De Stijl* (The Style), was highlighted in an exhibition at New York's Museum of Modern Art in 1932.

The following year the movement was repressed by the new Nazi regime in Europe, which caused the exodus of a number of significant architects to Britain's shores, including Marcel Breuer, Erno Goldfinger, Berthold Lubetkin, Erich (later Eric) Mendelsohn, and the two principals of the Bauhaus at Weimar and Dessau, Walter Gropius and Ludwig Mies van der Rohe. Some of these emigrés later moved on to live and work in the United States. Today, London enjoys the legacy of their influence.

The concept of Modernism was derived from its post-Russian Revolution social principles. Considered to be one of the bravest and most influential examples of Modernism in Britain is Mendelsohn and Serge Chermayeff's 'organic' De La Warr Pavilion at Bexhill. A delegation of visiting French mayors in the late 1930s remarked 'your seaside is socialism in practice'.

Ultimately, the very power that sought to destroy Great Britain unwittingly gave the nation a great gift, as these architects and designers brought their utopian dreams and a new spirit of architecture to enrich 'England's green and pleasant land'.

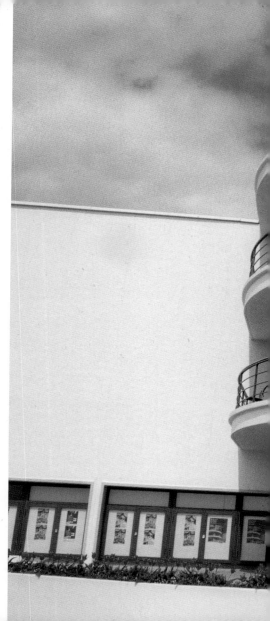

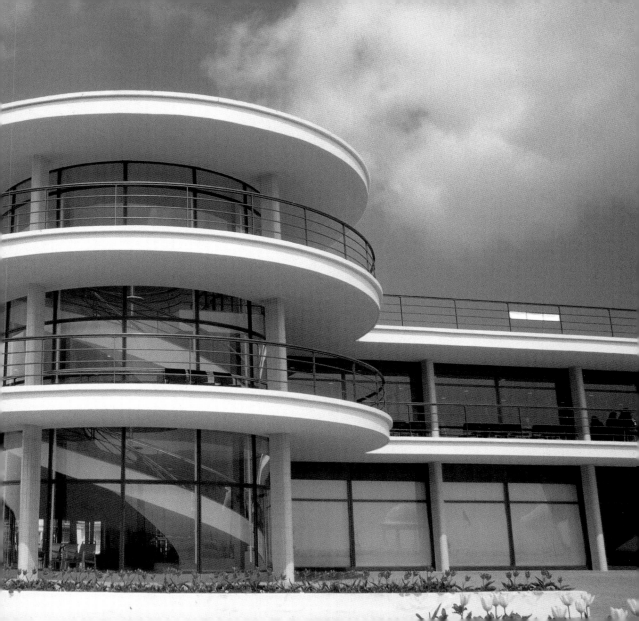

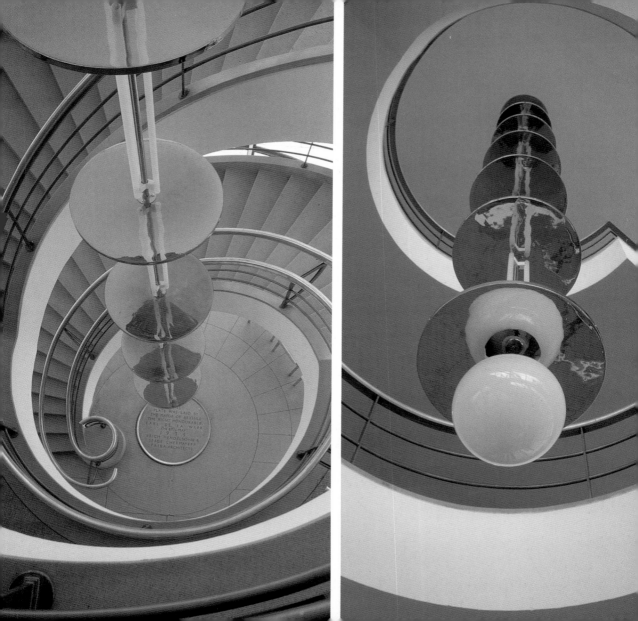